WAITING IN THE WING

JOSEPH KOBO
with
Gerry Finley-Day

WAITING IN THE WING

JOSEPH KOBO

The electrifying true story of a bishop who was once in the Military Wing of the ANC

WORD PUBLISHING
Nelson Word Ltd
Milton Keynes, England
WORD AUSTRALIA
Kilsyth, Australia
NELSON WORD CANADA
Vancouver, B.C., Canada
STRUIK CHRISTIAN BOOKS (PTY) LTD
Cape Town, South Africa
JOINT DISTRIBUTORS SINGAPORE –
ALBY COMMERCIAL ENTERPRISES PTE LTD
and
CAMPUS CRUSADE, ASIA LTD
PHILIPPINE CAMPUS CRUSADE FOR CHRIST
Quezon City, Philippines
CHRISTIAN MARKETING NEW ZEALAND LTD
Havelock North, New Zealand
JENSCO LTD
Hong Kong
SALVATION BOOK CENTRE
Malaysia

WAITING IN THE WING

<u>*Dedicated to*</u>

the late
Reverend Nicholas B. H. Bhengu

the man who
brought me to Christ

Contents

Foreword

*I*t is not often that one has the opportunity to meet someone like Joseph Kobo. Usually we have to be content with an Alistair MacLean story or Frederick Forsyth novel in which we encounter such characters. However, it was my privilege to meet Joseph Kobo two years ago, with his wife Mabel, and my admiration for them both will soon be seen to be justified by the reader of these enthralling pages. Not only do we move through political machinations and military exploits, but we encounter the Author of all stories, the God and Father of our Lord Jesus Christ, in the amazing way that Joseph was brought back to his Saviour while in solitary confinement.

As I am writing this foreword tremendous changes are happening in South Africa: all-race elections have taken place and President Mandela is addressing thousands of his countrymen outside the parliament building. Joseph's story, told in these pages, his current church-planting ministry and good-news service to the poor, along with the thousands of Christians in this new nation, will all play their part in the unfolding of a new chapter in this nation's history.

The God of the Bible who overruled and led an earlier Joseph through the political intrigues of Egypt, and also Jonah as he contended with the secular paganism of Assyria, is the same God who is at work in the world today, using men like Joseph Kobo who have the courage and vitality to stand up and be counted for Christ. It should be noted that God's overruling was also demonstrated through the seemingly insignificant prayers of a small church over the twenty-year period that Joseph was involved with the ANC.

I was thrilled and excited to read this moving book, which I think is strategic for God's purpose at this crucial time in South Africa. I trust that Joseph's story will have an ongoing ministry to everyone who believes in the God of the nations, who has given us good news for all the families of the earth.

Roger Forster
Ichthus Christian Fellowship

Abbreviations

ANC	African National Congress (South Africa)
BOSS	Bureau of State Security (South Africa)
'C' Squadron	Special Air Service (Rhodesia)
FRELIMO	Liberation Front (Mozambique)
KGB	Intelligence (Soviet Union)
MK	*Umkhonto we Sizwe* (Spear of the Nation)—ANC Military Wing (South Africa)
MOSSAD	Intelligence (Israel)
RENAMO	National Resistance (Mozambique)
RLI	Light Infantry (Rhodesia)
SADF	Defence Force (South Africa)
SB	Security Branch (South Africa)
SS	Selous Scouts (Rhodesia)
SWAPO	South West African People's Organisation (Namibia)
UNITA	Union for Total Independence (Angola)
ZANU	Mugabe's Patriotic Front (Rhodesia)
ZANLA	Military Wing of ZANU
ZAPU	Nkomo's Patriotic Front (Rhodesia)
ZIPRA	Military Wing of ZAPU

SOUTHERN AFRICA

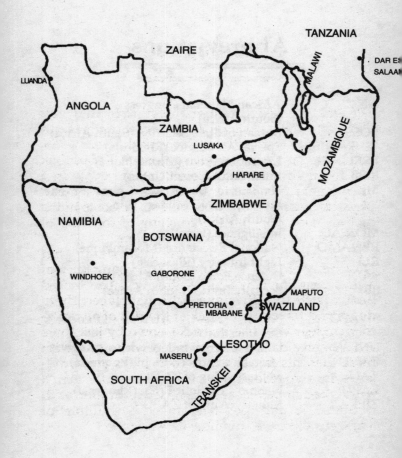

Prologue

It was, to misremember the start of that guy Dickens' *A Tale of Two Cities*, the worst of times and it *was* the worst of times. It was the year 1963. That was the year in which I, Joseph Kobo, took just too many blows and went reeling away in a brand-new direction. By blows I don't mean physical attacks; there were no fists or boots in the picture—not yet—but the crushing of so many of my hopes had been just about complete.

One of the blows had been the death that November of John F. Kennedy. The young buck of a president, the new King Arthur who had locked horns with the Russians, who had faced them down and forced them back at the risk of annihilatory nuclear war, had been cut down by just three ten-a-penny bullets. Kennedy, a white guy with more than his fair share of good looks and privileges in a goodlooking, privileged white man's world, had nonetheless symbolised aspiration with a capital 'A' and had been loved by millions of black guys like me, and now he was gone.

Another blow for me that year, as a South African black, had been our government's creation of 'independent Bantu homelands'—among them my own neck of the woods, Transkei, the land beyond the Kei river. The idea was that these lands would house the bulk of the black population while the white people kept the rest of the country for themselves. Of the twenty-odd million population, less than four million were actually white, yet they intended once and for all to hold onto territory twice the size of France. By comparison, Transkei added up to less than two Corsicas. The other homelands-to-be, Venda, Ciskei and Bophuthatswana, were even smaller.

Our government had timed their move in the slipstream of the African 'Wind of Change' as though to demonstrate that they, like the British, were finally dismantling their old ways. It was like telling the world they'd had their blacks as guests at a feast when we were really dogs in the corner thrown a scrap or two.

Another blow had been even closer to home; this same South African government had seized a certain black who was not only a Transkeian like me but a member of my own family, being my father's brother. He was called Nelson Mandela though his clan name was Rolihlahla to those of us of the Xhosa tribe. Rolihlahla—it meant 'Bridge-Puller' but could also translate as 'Problem-Causer'—was not only a Xhosa prince but also leader of the banned African National Congress party, and he was now a prisoner. Dramatically arrested, he had been taken to the South African version of Devil's Island—and although he had recently been brought back onto the mainland for trial it was obvious to guys like me that he would be returning to that piece of rock for years, if not for ever. Not only Rolihlahla Mandela, but almost the entire ANC leadership had been seized and thus swept from the board.

And then had come the even more personal blow to me, a man who in 1963 had proudly carried the title of Pastor Joseph Kobo. I was a minister with my own church and congregation. I had been a full-blooded Christian for nearly a decade, I had been enthusiastically baptised into the faith, had been married within it, had worked my heart out preaching it and that year I had waited. Waited for my superiors, the white bishops in the distant cities like Durban and Cape Town to challenge these government machinations on behalf of the weakest of their followers . . . but nothing had come.

In that latter part of the year it had finally dawned on me that no message, no counterplan, not even an acknowledgement would be forthcoming to any black rural church. It clicked that not only were the bishops not opposing these homelandisation notions—they were actually encouraging them. Scales of a sort fell from my eyes as I realised that, yes of course, they too were into this *apartheid*, this apartness-ideology. The

South African churches had been organised by them into separate units according to skin, after all. It was now obvious to me. Their 'all men equal in the sight of' preaching had been sheer hypocrisy. I, and plenty of other guys like me, had been tricked, used, Uncle Tom'd. Christianity was after all just a white man's religion, just as others, non-believers, had hissed to me all through the Fifties. And it wasn't so much Christianity these whites espoused, it was more the Old Testament than the New. Pride in the pioneering spirit, promised lands and chosen people was really all just a reflection of themselves. They'd never been really interested in the poor and the meek, didn't want to know much about the world of the underdog. But I did. Though I'd tried hard to transcend it, I was after all one myself. That lifelong inner awareness of something being badly wrong for black people came coursing through as never before.

That same winter, then, I made my decision. I was finished with pastoring, performing for the 'Dutch High Reformed' puppetmasters. I was angry, but not totally enraged. I would use my masters as they had used me. They had trained me well as a leader and a guide, so I'd use those talents to save Transkei and the other places from being shunted into oblivion. If I wasn't wanted in the lily-white flock I'd run with my own sort, even if they were thought of as packs. I made my move.

That December of 1963, the grass at Arlington Cemetery probably still crushed from all the

mourners, the *Robbeneiland* cell still a brief
experience to Mandela and the 'homelands' legisla-
tion all freshly and neatly filed, I took off my pastor's robes and changed into civilian clothes to
become a political animal. Even then, for all my
emotion, I didn't realise that I would one day put
on other clothing. I would have a camouflage suit
and AK-47 pouches furnished by John Kennedy's
arch enemies. I would jump from agitator to army
officer, from lieutenant to acting-commander in the
ANC's Military Wing, the *Umkhonto we Sizwe* or
Spear of the Nation. I would then be the most dangerous of predators to the flocks of the Western
world, a leading Communist-trained insurgent . . .
or, if you will, a top-ranking terrorist.

1

The Northern Border

*T*here were nine guys with me that day. This was thousands of days on from 1963. We were a team of trained guerrilla fighters, in military terms a cadre or in modern revolutionary terms a cell, though it was really the same basic ten-man formation that every army has built upon since Roman times. We had been out of South Africa for months and were now trying to infiltrate back across one of its borders.

I was the point-man. I had led them here, crawling and creeping all that morning to this designated jumpoff spot on the north bank of the Limpopo river. We were crouched right by the water but in the cover of dense trees . . . fever, acacia, mopane, mahogany. Their leaves blended with the 'rice-fleck' pattern of our East German camouflage suits. In moments, however, we would have to break cover and start across this river which was nearly half a kilometre in width. It was difficult to judge the exact distance; there had been no time for a previous reconnaissance and the operations officer back at base had planned from hazy recollection, knowing the topography would have changed over the months. The trees added to the confusion, their branches reaching right down to the water as though imitating the creatures we had watched coming to drink—the small bushbucks, the *hammerkops*, the furtive bigger things. The only sounds had been from the cicadas and the river itself. We had heard nothing else during our wait.

We were waiting for midday. The heat was the reason. Only black guys, we believed, could take noonday sun, whereas others usually retreated into shade, or rested, or were certainly at their least active. There was no sign of other men besides our group. We were formed into two lines, five on five. And they were all waiting for me. The guy right behind had only whispered two or three times before but now he whispered again.

'Nearly on the hour, Miwe.'

'Miwe' was my codename. I nodded, seeing no need to check my watch. I lifted my head slightly, to sniff for foreign smells again, and got nothing.

'OK, guys. Single file, numerical order.' I always gave my instructions in English though we were all Xhosa here; so much of our training had been in English. 'Keep right on my back, it's big enough.'

By big I really meant broad. I've always had a military build, not unlike a Sherman tank. I slid into the water. It was warm and muddy and I was up to my waist in seconds. I wouldn't go much deeper, I'd been told. This stretch was apparently a natural ford. As I waded further I heard the splash of number two man, a hand carelessly catching the surface. There was nothing in his hands, like mine. We had no pangas. I remember cursing that I hadn't broken off a branch to use as a staff or sounding-rod but the inevitable crack of wood might have carried too far. Despite the camouflage suits there wasn't a weapon amongst the ten of us, while a few miles downstream were gathered some of our opponents, probably the best-trained and best-armed troops in the whole of Africa.

The Beit Bridge, the only direct crossover point between South Africa and Zimbabwe, was in the seventies one of the most closely guarded stretches of water on the entire Dark Continent. Then, the other country was called Rhodesia and white soldiers were manning either end of the structure. Named after one of Cecil Rhodes' co-adventurers, the bridge has fourteen spans in all over the 414 metres of river, with small hamlets built around the inevitable customs houses. In those days they were fortified hamlets.

The bridge's guards were, it had been estimated, of around company strength each side, meaning around three hundred men. There was also a constant northward flow of supplies and 'volunteers' from South Africa. Round the structure itself were pillboxes, machine-gun emplacements and acres of barbed wire. All the approaches had been turned into a miniature desert, every bit of foliage including the spectacular baobab trees cleared so that nobody could advance unseen.

In addition to the infantry there would be crews manning armoured vehicles with Africanised names such as 'Hippos' and 'Rhinos'. Below the bridge in the river, more wire was unfurled against climbers and there were nets strung out to catch any floating mines. High above, the sky was covered too. A few miles south of the bridge, at Messina, there was an airstrip, with another at Sentinel to the northwest. Helicopters or aeroplanes would be formed up there, we knew. Perhaps there would even be ancient Dakota DC3s which, as other guerrilla cadres had learnt to their cost, could drop men on top of you before you realised what was happening.

There were thus in the very close vicinity far too many soldiers of Dutch, British, German, French and latterly Portuguese stock, all of whom we knew simply as 'the Boer'. The standard armament for these men was the FN, either the self-loading rifle or the general-purpose machine-gun. The range of either weapon was such that it could sweep the full width of the Limpopo if required. A burst of their 7.62 millimetre bullets could chop almost anything in half, maybe even a mahogany tree. Certainly a mahogany man.

But that day we were not in the least bit

interested in the Beit Bridge. We were not sabo-
teurs but infiltrators. The camouflage clothing was
our only military accoutrement, worn solely to
insert us onto home soil whereupon, in the classic
guerrilla move, we would simply peel off into
civilian clothes and melt into the local black civilian population. At that moment in time, though,
our suits were obvious enemy uniforms, a red rag
to any Boer soldier, should there be contact. But
they hadn't seen us, surely. We were far enough
up-stream and only the river itself was growling.
The wildlife on the banks had disappeared only
because they had sensed us, and not because of
whites. Nobody was watching me through sights,
nobody had defected and informed, I was sure. All
the same, I almost jumped when the guy behind
gave another whisper.

'Miwe, second wave'll be coming up soon,
remember.'

I didn't need reminding. We all knew another
ten-man cadre was following in our wake, with
about an hour between us, and behind that another
team. It was planned that thirty of us in all were to
slip through this one day. I tried to wade faster,
though we were still under the canopy of leaves. I
knew my nine guys would have their eyes fixed on
my back and I tried to be as rocklike as possible. I
didn't think anyone saw, but after jumping at number two man I had begun to shudder. It wasn't
Boer guns I had become fearful of. It was something more . . . you might call it home-grown. I

wondered how many of those wading guys behind knew.

I had discovered only a day before that this fordable stretch of the Limpopo had always been a very lonely area, and lonely for a very good reason. It was notorious for the high infestation of a certain creature. Not only did I know the English and African name for this beast, but after university education on either side of the European continent, I even knew the scientific term. In Latin it was *Niloticus*. It was the African crocodile.

It was, as the name infers, originally known as the Nile crocodile; even the Romans never knew how much of Africa there was and how many of the things there might be. The ones on our continent are among the largest in the world. Some are twelve feet in length, sometimes sixteen, and the weight can exceed a ton. In central and southern Africa it is a reptile more feared than even the mamba.

The crocodile moves like a submarine, eyes periscoping into the air for an instant to fix on its target and then closing in underwater with no telltale disturbance, whereas even a shark's fin gives some warning. Muddy African water helps its hunting. Its main tactic is to surge up and seize, then immediately thrust back into deeper water, straightaway rolling over and over both to unbalance its prey and to lose it any height advantage. Another trick is to tail-flick the target into its jaws.

Even in Transkei far to the south we'd had to watch our cattle and once I'd just missed seeing a buffalo taken.

Now this area was apparently alive with the things—the Limpopo is also known as the Crocodile River—and I couldn't see more than a few inches into the water around me. I kept glancing down, though I made my head as straight as possible so the guys wouldn't realise. Suddenly the water changed, lightened and then it was dazzling. We were out of tree cover and into the open. I found myself looking left, right and left again as though crossing a Cape Town street. There was nothing but more greenery curving away in either direction, no boats, no men. The river was now a flickering golden mirror in my face, though still stopping me seeing what was underwater. I waded on, still waistdeep, more the rock than ever. Was there some warning a crocodile gave, I wondered, some sound the beast emitted? Why hadn't our High Command used a local guy as guide instead of me? Maybe there hadn't been one available.

I took another step and the water was suddenly on my chest. My camouflage was now almost black with water and sweat and getting tighter. We should have been issued rubber wetsuits, I thought—and why was the water deeper? Had there been a rainstorm while we were on the march the day before? I shoved my chest on and tried not to think of problems, or reptiles—only to remember another story. In a nearby tributary of this very river there had reputedly lived a python god to whom a local tribe sacrificed young maidens. The thought disappeared as I remembered a more contemporary danger. The sky above. We were now totally exposed to it and I should be watching out for aerial activity. Hopefully a guy behind had been looking as we'd waded. I craned. The sky was that light blue, the colour of some Boers' eyes. There was no sign of Boer planes or choppers, though, not even vapour-trails in the stratosphere. The only hovering things apart from the half-invisible insects were plover, the birds that apparently hung around crocodiles to pick their teeth for them.

I brought my gaze straight ahead and started to walk on tiptoe. The far bank's trees were at last coming closer. I recognised most as mopane—I had once worked in the forestry industry. But I was a very different person now, a hardened and trained soldier. I'd had Marxist-Leninist instruction to the point of being 'brainwashed' and should be without fear and yet . . . there was this subliminal awareness. Next second I was in under my head. I choked, pulled back and my boots slipped on the unseen riverbed. My knee was touched by something and I backtracked to chest-level. I heard a worried grunt and someone else tried to whisper my name but I didn't look round. I realised I had momentarily wandered from the ford. I moved on, angry with myself but gaining strength from the moment. I was completely soaked but I hadn't been a drowning man. Nothing of my past life had flashed before me.

But OK, if you should really want to know, my life had begun in 1935. I was a genuine New Year baby, born on January the first, so I was to get a full twelve-month span straight away. Funnily, or rather unfunnily, enough 1935 was the year that saw military action returning to sub-Saharan Africa for the first time since the Great War, with the Italians invading Abyssinia. I was born a very typical Xhosa child in a typical *rondavel* or round-house in the village of Basire, about fifteen miles from Umtata, the capital of Transkei. My father, a cattle farmer, was delighted to have another son and therefore another helper for his herd. Hence my clan name Zoleseli meaning 'Soul-Comforter'; with a boy and a girl already in the family another of the latter had been dreaded. My Christian name reflected the family's nominal Anglicanism. As soon as I had been able to walk—barefoot of course—I'd been taken out to work amongst the cattle and given my knobkerry, my herder's stick, which would change and lengthen as I did.

My early days were peaceful, pastoral—idyllic, I suppose. There were endless grassy green hills broken only by the whites and browns of the villages and the cattle, with just a few other creatures. If you wanted change you could saunter east to the 'Wild Coast' and gaze out at the deep-blue Indian

Ocean, or you could turn west to the Drakensberg range—MY mountains as I soon thought of them—with their distant snowy peaks. And of course there were some white faces around; at first just other farmers, traders and policemen but as I grew to five, more such men appeared. These men were soldiers in khaki uniforms.

Men of my own tribe, my own village, began wearing that same khaki. I was vaguely aware of things happening somewhere else. It's always said that South Africa is like a world on its own, such is its size and varied landscape, but I began hearing of strange places and people. I watched troops training, saw massed aeroplanes above. I heard my father talk. Some of our tribe were going away. They were off to places like Abyssinia to help take on the Italians, and then going even further north in Africa. I saw exciting newsreels at our small local cinema.

One day I heard news which made war less exciting; four hundred local men, Xhosas enlisted in the South African army, had been lost on a troopship which sank. On a summer's day in 1942 I heard of the terrible fall of the town called Tobruk with its mainly South African garrison. There were other tragic places outside our continent—the name Russia kept recurring. And there was this America, which seemed to mean exciting things. Perhaps it was the sheer volume and importance of world events at that time that awakened a deep thirst for knowledge in me, but awakened I was.

I had started school at seven in the small school but I did well straight away for a cattle farmer's son. I kept questioning my teacher and he kept having to open his atlas. He pointed out the Rome our Springboks had helped take and the Berlin our allies were nearing. By the time the war was over I was hooked on study and spending more time indoors than out in the kraals. I was an unlikely-looking bookworm though; I had a naturally powerful build, always did well on the sports field and any fights I got into I usually won. I also knew very early on that using your brain always gave you an extra edge.

By the time I was nearly fourteen I had attained 'Standard Six', the highest grade in primary school, which allowed you to go on to higher education. And then my father stepped in. I'd done enough, he said. I didn't need further education because I'd be following in his footsteps like my brother. We were simple country folk, we had no real money. I couldn't be supported at a college or university. Get those fancy ideas out of your head, I was told. Settle down to life as you know it. In a classic father–son confrontation he even threatened me with his large drover's stick if I didn't see sense. I didn't. In a far from original move I decided to run away from home. I didn't go mad-bull though, but I used my head all the same. I carefully folded away my two pass certificates—in case my father tore them up—and planned. A cousin of mine had also done well at school and with money in his immediate family, was going off to college in Bloemfontein, to a place called Hill Down.

The whole village was going to see him off on the train. I went along too. I did more than that. At the country station on the East London line I slipped aboard the train while nobody in the crowd was looking. I had no suitcases. I was wearing my usual work clothes: old shorts, shirt, blanket, no shoes. But I had my two precious pass certificates, those and my drover's stick which I carried wherever I went.

By the time I was discovered we were well out of Transkei. My mortified cousin and the conductor tried to put me off at the next station. I dug my heels in, even though they were bigger than me. My cousin took over from the shrugging official and tried to be clever. He explained he only had funds for himself, not a penny extra. He told me to take a good look at my reflection in the carriage window. I didn't bother. I sat back down, determined. We finally got to Bloemfontein and my cousin boxed clever again. He gave me the slip at the huge station, probably thinking a callow country boy like me would become disoriented, lose his nerve and leap back on the next train home. I didn't. I walked out of the station into the big city streets, still barefoot, and asked the way to Hill Down College.

I remember it was a long walk past tall buildings and I'd never seen so many cars. There were so many white folk around. The black people too looked different, smart and urbanised, and I saw plenty of heads shaking. Even to them I must have looked like a wild thing. They must have seen me coming a long way off at Hill Down. The boys there were all black, too, but in neat clothes, pressed shorts, long socks and real leather shoes. They had been playing football outside so it must have been break-time. All I could do was smooth my blanket into a plaid over my shoulder, grip my stick and take a deep breath, then go in.

Heads had already turned. I could see teeth grinning in the sun but they weren't welcoming grins. I heard voices in English and Xhosa. 'I like his shoes,' somebody said. Within minutes the football game was forgotten and they were all around me like a pack of hyenas. My plaid was tugged at. A big kid pushed to the fore. He was a Xhosa like me but at least a year older and a foot taller. He was a leader type and he was leading the laughs and jeering. I thought he was going to stamp on my bare feet. He had a cruel look. I felt tired after the long train journey, tired and suddenly angry. The big kid now pointed at my knobkerry and made as if to snatch it. I saw red. I'd used the stick all the time back at home, both to discipline cattle and in playfights with pals. The big kid pressed in, his hands and feet threatening, and all of a sudden I was wielding my stick in both hands, low down. I hit the big kid hard across his skull. Blood came streaming out of his hair the next second. The gang of boys around me suddenly went as quiet as mice. I stood swinging my stick a moment, turning in a circle to all comers, but none of them moved. Then I heard feet running, heavier feet. Teachers were coming to sort out this unknown little savage.

I was now more than halfway across the Limpopo, still soaking from head to foot but glistening like a beacon to the guys behind me. That the added luminosity might be even more attractive to something underwater was another concern. I waded on, glancing around for a sign of eyes or scaly skin or teeth. Old hunters say that if you're ever attacked in the bush by a lion or cheetah and are weaponless, you can as a last resort literally chance your arm and thrust straight down the throat to choke it just before the jaws close, and maybe scare it off. Not so in the case of a river crocodile. It would be back next second for the rest of you. With no stick around, the best I could try would be a quick punch thrown between the eyes if I was fast enough. The idea of clamping the jaws shut with an armlock was too fanciful even though I'd used the grip in bar-room brawls. I shut out the image and looked at the trees. Still no Boer soldiers were among them. Why not? They too must know about the *crokodil* stories. Maybe that was why they had no guards here, the beasts being their sentries.

But still nothing was happening and I was still up only to my chest, no, my ribcage now. The water was getting shallow. We were three-quarters of the way across. I wanted to turn to reassure the nine spattered faces but I knew all they wanted was a rock-man. And then as I started to home in on the bank it hit me. We were in fact at the most dangerous spot. Crocodiles wouldn't have been swimming in midstream but basking on dry land and were maybe all set to streak in. We were under tree cover again now. I couldn't make out details among the trunks and bushes. Twenty, thirty metres. This was maybe the crucial bit. Maybe a line of the things were watching. Maybe we should break and run. The water was at the waist now. Maybe I should lead a fast rush in and beat the hidden reptiles before they launched themselves on us. On dry land we would be among them and able to use our height, use our feet in their jump-boots. No, no wild last-minute rushes, I decided.

The water receded further. I fixed on one thick treetrunk ahead as if it was a flagpole and started to march as though back in my main Zambian base. I marched *at* it. I heard the others mimic me and try to fall into step. I came into real shallows, thighs and then knees surfacing, and I could hear

the rhythm of our marching. Far too dangerous a
sound. I raised my hand for halt, listened and
then, sure nothing was watching and waiting on
the bank, I made the fan-out signal. Then we were
into cool shade and our boots were no longer slip-
pery and the only things shying away from us
were small nonreptilians. Doubled up, we climbed
the bank and moved to the edge of the trees. There
were mopanes everywhere but we also saw one
huge baobab. It was thick bush, typical of the
northern Transvaal. Number two man said his first
words in South African air:

'Twenty past twelve, Miwe.'

Minutes or hours, I wasn't sure. I thought of
the teams behind. We had to move. We slid just
out of tree cover for another ten minutes, letting
our suits dry and lighten in colour again. Then
after checking that all to the south seemed quiet
and there seemed nothing on my flanks, I led the
crawl into the bush. One hour later we were
pulling off the suits and burying them in a deep
hole, too deep for animals to unearth. We had been
well-trained in caching. We would move on to the
southeast. It was the ploughing season here and
now we could appear in a field and look like harmless black farmworkers. My destination was
Venda, one of the homeland areas, and it meant a
few more trained men were back home and in
position. By dusk of that day I had dispersed the
entire team safely, in ones and twos. I had watched

the last man being welcomed into a kraal in the last
good light.

It was some days later when I learned what
had happened to Team Two, the cadre in our wake.
I never knew the full facts. Perhaps they made a
late jumpoff. Perhaps the worst of the day's heat
was over and Boer soldiers had become active and
launched a random patrol or perhaps an aircraft
had made a sweep at just the wrong time. That
second group was spotted and wiped out to a man,
probably by FN guns. It must have been sheer bad
luck, for had it been a primed ambush the Boers
would have been after all three waves. They
would have taken us first in silence—me first, of
course. Then it would have been a game of one by
one. As it was, we'd got through and the final
wave was warned off and fell back to try again
another day. Maybe the crocodiles of the river did
make an appearance, attracted by blood and
bodies. The Boer soldiers were, as always, too
good and we were, we knew, no match for them.
But to try and do just that one day, match them,
was the job of *Umkhonto* officers like me. I'd have
to keep leading infiltrations to put enough men
and weaponry on the ground. That was why
they'd given me that codename. Miwe means 'He
Who Crosses Over'.

2

The Kalahari Run

*T*ears of pain were running down that big kid's face along with the blood when the college teachers came across the playground and disarmed me of my drover's stick. I was frogmarched into the buildings, to an office marked 'Principal'. The man himself was at his desk and he looked astounded. Me, I felt angry more than anything, and wanted the stick back. The Principal stood up, towered over me and my bare feet and clenched fists, and then with a half-smile started the obvious questions. I put my hand in my pocket and had my wrist grabbed. Another teacher thought I was going for a knife. I finally got out my two pass certificates and they were spread out on the desk.

The Principal's new smile took me off guard. I was disarmed for the second time, sort of. Suddenly tearful, I started telling the simple truth. I meant no harm. I wanted to learn, learn everything they could teach me. Was it possible? The other teachers stared at my old plaid and shorts, my brother's hand-me-downs, and looked at one another.

The Principal—he was black and Xhosa and in a white flannel suit—reached for the telephone on his desk. I'd only seen phones like that at stores and police stations. I thought, he's phoning the police. He was using that gutteral Afrikaans which I'd heard policemen use. He looked at me, giving a description. Then we waited and he offered me a drink. I only wanted water. Then into the school playground came this big gleaming car, a white man at the wheel. He wasn't in a uniform though. He had dusty clothes and a big sunhat like Boer farmers wore. And a Boer farmer was exactly what he was. But I'll call him my Gentleman farmer, because that's also exactly what he was.

He happened to be from one of the oldest and most powerful Afrikaner families in the Bloemfontein area. He was broad, like me even then, but tall and with those light eyes that have to crinkle most of the time in African sunlight. His face crinkled day and night, with smiles. I found out later he wasn't only a leading farmer but a leading Christian. I found myself smiling back and maybe it helped. He seemed to decide something. He got the Principal to get in touch with my family back in Transkei. If they agreed, I could stay here and start college. Everything would be paid for. This white farmer would pay for it. Even the Principal looked surprised at such decisiveness.

As it dawned that I was looking at a patron out

of the blue, and my education would be completely taken care of, I came near to cracking, breaking down again. All this kindness, this help, what could I do in return? The Gentleman looked over at my stick and smiled. I could help on his farm in my spare time for a start. I got back the stick. The kid it had hit had been treated, the bleeding stopped. The farmer gave me a reproachful smile, but another smile. Maybe he thought I'd proved I had clout.

That afternoon I was at the man's farm, meeting his wife and then all three of us were in Bloemfontein and I was being bought school equipment and clothes and, for the first time in my life, shoes. And then back at the farm I met his kids home from school. They were around my age and we became friends straight away. Black guys on the farm were treated like family too, even though they were paid workers. My Gentleman, I soon discovered, was a capital-'L' Liberal who had always favoured multiracialism and for all his personal privileges was a vehement opponent of white supremacy. Maybe there was a personal reason away back in his family's history—I was never told. But this being the mid-1940s, the man was probably regarded as an eccentric, if not a madman, by his peers. For me, he was one of the greatest men I would ever meet. His church was mixed, which was how he and the Principal of Hill Down College were pals. He was pals with many blacks, and my own father would soon be one. I now had a second family, was almost an adopted son. One of his own sons would later become a leading liberal politician in South Africa. When I knew him, he was just a playmate. We would play sports, go hunting together.

I was therefore given a privileged insight, virtually unknown for most South African black kids in the immediate post-war years. I learnt both at college and back at this new home. I learnt about Europe and its arts and sciences. I devoured his library, which contained Dickens, Dumas, Rider Haggard and R. L. Stevenson. On the gramophone I listened to Bach and 'van Beethoven', the Austrian with the Boer-like name. I learned to shoot, to handle guns, and I learnt another skill that would stand me in good stead.

My Gentleman had umpteen cars of all sorts—saloons, estates, pickups—which were parked all over the farm, as on farms the world over. The keys would usually be left in the ignition. It didn't take me long to realise that around me were readily-available playthings. Soon I was starting up, trying the gears, using the pedals. I'd lurch back and forth, not daring to actually drive. I'd try another vehicle, and another, like a child with too many toys. Until the day I was reversing and I glanced in the mirror . . . to find my Gentleman watching from a barn. I happened to be in his own car, a brand-new Studebaker Land Cruiser. I froze and stalled it. I'd been to see that Disney film and felt just like the Sorcerer's Apprentice. I crept out

40

of the advanced nylon upholstery and waited. His boots marched nearer and with them I was sure would come the word 'ungrateful', but nothing was said. He simply got into his car, still with the ignition on, restarted it and drove away. I didn't know where to put myself or show myself.

I kept away even from his wife. When he returned later that afternoon he had someone with him. It was another white guy, an old farmhand who drove the heavy vehicles and the tractors. They pulled up nearby, and my Gentleman pointed at me and spoke in Afrikaans which I could now understand. 'See that boy, Anni,' he said. 'Teach him, OK. You teach him good.'

I had of course been given corporal punishment by my own father in Transkei and I guess my Gentleman as my patron was entitled to mete it out if he wanted to, or even to appoint others to do the deed. I waited unresisting, head hung.

'Yeah,' the farmer continued, 'You teach him how to drive everything, everything in sight, tractors too, because otherwise any day now he's going to smash up my shiny new Stoodie.'

I wasn't yet fourteen, years away from a legal licence.

By the 1970s I was possibly one of the most experienced drivers in the whole of southern Africa.

Which was why the *Umkhonto* High Command had decided that a goodly proportion of my 'crossings' should be motorised.

There were two of us this time. The other man's codename was Nomuula—'Rainy Season'. We were taking turns at the wheel because we were on a long run. We were running guns—AK-47 assault carbines and their twenty-round magazines—for deposition at a cache. They were all in the back of our vehicle, a 1975 Toyota pickup which, like that Studebaker, also called itself a Land Cruiser. The guns were under a huge pile of cattle hides. A strip of hide was wrapped round each gun in case the pile as a whole came adrift or dislodged in the rough terrain. Our route was a deliberately slow and leisurely one that took us through the Kalahari, a vast desert that in turn spilt over from a neighbouring country called Botswana which, though having long left the church, I thought of as 'Blessed' Botswana.

Formerly called Bechuanaland, the country has always looked like a huge unwanted pack on South Africa's back, a pack she has never been able to remove because of international constraints, although a few pulls and pokes happened every so often. To the *Umkhonto* Botswana was an ideal bolthole. A quarter of a million square miles of near-emptiness with a tiny population and a landscape largely as dry as a bone, but the place was a positive thirst-quencher to guys like me.

It was into Botswana that Nelson Mandela had slipped in 1962, to undertake his extensive tour of Africa including military training, and Botswana

had been his springboard back into South Africa,
though his arrest far to the south had come just a
few weeks later. At that time it had still been a
British colony dating back to the Zulu wars, but
Botswana had finally achieved its independence in
1966. Neighbouring Rhodesia had already taken
that step, illegally, and Botswana immediately
became a 'Frontline' state not only for *Umkhonto*
but a mass of other liberation movements.

Gaborone the capital was soon housing ANC
offices alongside the high commissions and
embassies. Despite that, the Botswanan premier
Seretse Khama was treading a tightrope with his
reliance on neighbouring white countries for jobs
and exports. Khama was in fact married to an
Englishwoman. Deals had been struck, but part of
the bargain was that the Botswanans had South
African 'protection', meaning a very close guard on
the country's borders. The Boers had looked at
their maps and seen that Botswana was an ideal
site for Ho Chi Minh-style trails from other
committed countries like Zambia—which was
exactly the case. Men and munitions would filter
through in various ways, sometimes in one fell
swoop, sometimes in relays with plainclothes pickup teams.

Nomuula and I were such a team that day. It
was a typically searing morning and we were
almost straddling the border in an area where the
Kalahari kept any idea of boundaries undefined. I
was again playing the noonday sun game, hoping

the Boers were less than a hundred per cent alert. We had been switching from one desert trail to another as though lost. The landscape was really semi-desert, with plenty of vegetation, although there were still plenty of dunes and hummocks of red sand. The idea was that we had come from the Gaborone area, or rather the huge Lobatse abattoir on its outskirts, and had bought the cattle hides cheaply with a view to making a profit in some South African market. In fact we were headed for a cache-site in Bophuthatswana, another of the so-called 'homelands'.

As the morning wore on the heat had affected even the pair of us. The sand seemed to permanently shimmer and we'd hardly seen any wild animals. We hadn't even caught sight of a single Bushman. I had driven since sunrise, after making the usual vehicle checks, the checks which Anni the old farmhand had taught me to make on any machine before use. Not that this Toyota needed much attention; it had been chosen because of its reputation for Japanese reliability and purchased in another part of South Africa with ANC funds. All the same, I had topped up the water, loaded the spare jerrycans, checked the fuel, wiped the dipstick and had even checked the brand-new tyres. The last thing a gun-run needed was a puncture, hence the expensive Michelins. And whereas in other countries such good tyres on an otherwise humble workhorse might have attracted attention, the fierce legalism of the Boers worked for us; poor treads meant very heavy fines for blacks or whites, so everyone made it their business to have more than up-to-scratch rubber around their wheels.

With little to worry about and the heat blazing through the screen, I decided to let Nomuula take the wheel and have forty winks. We were still meandering over dirt-tracks but moving slowly south. Nomuula climbed into the right-hand side of the cab—South Africans still drive as in the UK. Nomuula was in his early twenties and had been trained at a base in Zambia like me, reaching the rank of sergeant. We were both in old cotton overalls. He was a good enough driver, if a bit on the fast side, and I'd warned him about speeding. He also liked American soul music played loudly and that seemed to influence his driving. As I preferred the classics and I was a full lieutenant, I had told him to shut the radio-cassette off and had been obeyed. Then, gently bouncing over the desert, I drifted off to sleep.

I woke up with a lurch and heard a loud jangling song. The glare was worse than ever and I was about to shout at Nomuula when I realised the music was not coming from our cab. We were in a queue of cars and on a tarmacked road, though red sand was still all around. We had come onto a proper highway and the music was coming from the car ahead, its windows wide open in the heat. The car was a Peugeot estate and in it was a white family, a woman and kids. I rubbed my face, looked behind us over the pile of hides and saw a big Mercedes truck braking. I swung back to the Peugeot and saw two or three more roofs, and then I was wide awake and cold as ice.

Two khaki Landrovers, police Landrovers, were parked in an arrowhead blocking the road. They had obviously set up a random checkpoint. A large van was being scrutinised. The driver was on the road, his papers being checked. He was black, but so were several of the policemen. The rest of the queue was edging up slowly.

Nomuula noticed I was no longer asleep. 'Comrade, Comrade Miwe,' he began, trying to explain the situation. He always used the political prefix.

'I see,' I whispered back in the Xhosa he'd used. 'Easy, Nomuula. Slow down, you're a bit near to this car.'

I tried to be calm but it had the opposite effect. I saw his knee jump and hit the gearstick. He'd gone into the wrong gear.

'That's four-wheel. Into second.'

Again his knee hit the gears. I saw his whole thigh shaking. He was panicking. His face, badly scarred from an old untreated infection, was a mask of sweat and his eyes were on stalks. He was high, too high. There was no smell of beer or dagga in the cab. It was just uncontrolled adrenalin.

'Easy, dammit, Nomuula.' I switched to English.

He gave a nod and went into first. I thought

he'd pulled himself together, but there came a shout ahead from the big van, some altercation. I saw Nomuula's hand go inside his overalls and up to his armpit where I knew his handgun was. For personal protection we had been issued with 9mm Makarov automatics, but only as a last resort. Mine was in the glove compartment, but I'd seen him position his weapon in an inner pocket as though shoulderholstered. He'd watched too many American thrillers; I remembered his enthusing about the Shaft films. Now his scarred profile was looking left and right, where there was no barrier. I read his mind. Make a run for the open desert, he was thinking. And if the Landrovers take off in pursuit, empty the Makarov back at them.

'Nomuula, don't do anything. Watch it, you're starting to creep forward. Watch the Peugeot. We're OK—we've got papers, remember.'

He braked but he was hardly listening, his eyes again going to the desert. For a moment I wondered if I was being too casual in my reactions and then I saw a strange moving speck on the sand. I blinked. It wasn't an animal. Kalahari animals weren't black. I realised what it was. I turned in my seat, twisted down and looked up through the rear cab window. Almost directly above us, there hovered a light military helicopter. The moving speck was its shadow. It was an Alouette 3. I had been on an aircraft identification course in another Frontline state. Its crew were surveying the line of vehicles, probably taking a good look at our load of

47

cattle-hides. They'd have a pair of extra hides too if we wrongfooted ourselves.

'Nomuula, we can't do a damn thing. Chopper right above us. You hear?'

'Ahead, Comrade Miwe. They're moving, van's going.'

Sure enough the police were waving on the big vehicle after a search; I remembered that very recently a pantechnicon had been halted and had been found to contain four *Umkhonto* men. Maybe they were just after large vehicles and they were hurrying the cars ahead as though zeroing on us. Nomuula revved and crunched the gears and his leg came alive again.

'Sergeant Nomuula, do–'

It all happened fast. The jangling music from the Peugeot faded as it drove off, there came an impatient honk from the truck behind and I heard the Alouette rotors for the first time. With the change of background noise, Nomuula went into action, the Makarov coming out and the driving hand hauling on the wheel. I knew that even if the Alouette didn't have a gunner it would never let go of us until ground reinforcements closed in. I knew what to do. I lifted, chopped his hand off the wheel and then flicked the gear into neutral so we couldn't go anywhere. Then I grabbed him and lifted him right off the seat, so hard and fast his head hit the roof. While he was still in the air I slid myself underneath, over the gears and into his position. The Makarov was in his other hand but I

48

managed to get a knee to it and it dropped from his grasp onto the floor. Then somehow I was flinging him hard, very hard, to the other side of the cab, so his head hit metal again. Then I was in second and the wheel was straightened. The Peugeot was passing the checkpoint and I wasn't sure whether the police had seen the violent movement in our cab. I looked at Nomuula's scarred, shocked face and had another idea.

'The radio, full up, full up.'

He shook himself and punched the button. On came a burst of music, maybe it was James Brown, maybe Osibisa, I don't remember. It filled the cab and I jumped up and down at the wheel in time.

I saw Nomuula look for his gun, just as my heel found it and kicked it into cover, despite the risk of the thing going off.

'Your head, jig your head too. Come on.'

The kids in the Peugeot had heard the music and their heads were jigging and they were smiling back at us. But they were also going and we were slowing beside the checkpoint. I saw a blonde girl wave goodbye.

And then the police were waving at us too. Waving us on. There were six of them and they looked tired and hot, even the black ones. One of the latter grinned at our music though, while a frecklefaced Boer glared and mouthed the words *'Donner kaffirs'*, 'Damned blackies'.

And then we were through. Nomuula had an angry bruise starting over his scars and he did a

49

doubletake back, spotting the Alouette for the first time.

'It's not following, is it, Sergeant?' I asked him.

He shook his head. 'I'm sorry, Comrade Miwe, for not handling myself.'

I told him it was OK, though I didn't give him the Makarov back until later. I did all the driving for the remainder of that run into Bophuthatswana. After the caching of the guns I never drove with Nomuula again, in fact I never drove with anyone else. It would always be just me at the wheel.

I suppose I had lived up to my own codename again, though that time I'd really only just 'crossed over' from the passenger seat.

3

The Sudan

O ur military wing *Umkhonto*, sometimes abbre-
viated to MK, had been activated on 16 December
1961, which was also the precise date of a famous
1834 Boer victory over an African tribe. That date
was further familiar to historians as Hitler's final
shock counter-offensive, which had led to the
Battle of the Bulge in Western Europe. Here in
South Africa the *Umkhonto's* offensiveness had
been strictly limited; we, unlike Hitler, were not
waging all-out war and the ground to be gained
was purely political. A few bombed buildings in
Johannesburg and Durban hardly constituted a
major campaign. For a start, the trained people on
the ground at that time were far too few . . . which
had been exactly the design of the Pretoria government. Black guys, as Nelson Mandela was soon to
articulate, had deliberately been denied military
experience by not having been conscripted after
1945. The desperate days of World War II when
any helping hand had been welcomed were now
long forgotten. The only way to even the odds

therefore had been to slip out of South Africa and train elsewhere, as Mandela had done.

Originally this had meant the other end of Africa—Algeria, Ethiopia and Egypt—but as the sixties had turned into the seventies the game had changed, as all games do in the Dark Continent more than anywhere else. Ben Bella had been overthrown, as had Haile Selassie. Nasser had gone by natural causes but his successor Sadat was, after the Yom Kippur defeat, casting around for new friends with less support for people like the distant ANC. New players had moved in, however—the Young Colonels. There was Qaddafi of Libya, who with revolutionary fervour was providing training facilities in his vast deserts not only for African liberation movements but for guerrillas from every other continent . . . and there was also support from Sudan's Colonel, al-Numeiri.

Sudan had always been an important prize for us, and Mandela, when at liberty years before, had secured promises from one of Numeiri's predecessors, promises which had been honoured. Though we were grateful to Qaddafi, Sudan, because of its geographical position, was the better staging-post. Sudan was the ideal conduit for arms and supplies coming across the Mediterranean from the Black Sea. The Eastern bloc—and nobody else—was equipping us. We were of course, as any steely Pentagon general would have termed it, 'doing the Commie thing'. And yet the idol of any such general, Winston Churchill, had once so sought

Russian help he had compared it with giving the devil a favourable reference. For their part, the Soviets and their satellites were still playing the Great Game of Czarist days, of nibbling where they could at Western influence . . . and yet in Africa events would always be coloured by the landscape and the actual men on the ground. For many, it was more a sport, more the 'Big Game'.

I was certainly an enthusiastic player that day in the mid-seventies when, as an officer freshly trained in logistics, I boarded a flight to the Sudan to oversee one of our Ho Chi Minh trails. I had taken off from an international airport other than a South African one. I had of course slipped out of the country illegally into a Frontline state, where the local ANC office had furnished me with a passport supplied by the United Nations. I had taken off over greenery that had become darker and more equatorial until I had dozed off. The glare must have woken me. I looked out my porthole and the world had turned burnt yellow. It was nothing like the coppery Kalahari. I was staring at the big-as-the-moon Sahara. For hours I seemed to stare at nothing but sand. Because of it I couldn't work out our jet's height. There seemed to be nothing but yellowness.

'It's growing too, Comrade Miwe. The Sahara is moving south all the time, little by little, year by year.' The man in the next seat, a Sudanese attaché who was my escort, broke the cabin's hum with his comment in fluent English. 'Desertification, they call it. Maybe it will reach your country one day. We are of course used to it.'

It was a depressing thought for a guy like me used to green grass and the Indian Ocean, but almost immediately I bucked up. I spotted a thin blue line that widened and began to glisten.

'The Nile.'

The attaché nodded with a smirk; he was an Arab and wore a similar safari suit to mine, safaris being a sort of mufti to military personnel. I remembered that Mandela himself had come this way and walked along the banks of that Nile. And now—I gave a heavy sigh—he was still at this very moment back in that sea-surrounded prison back on the Cape. The Nile grew and widened as the jet began a descent. And then there was a white glimmer ahead. The glimmer became solid and I was reminded of bleached picked-clean bones. Minarets began rising in pairs, by the dozens. I noticed a haze of either smoke or dust or both, meaning thousands upon thousands of human beings engrossed in the business of life. The jet circled back to the south, going lower over suburbs. I took in more of the capital of the largest country in Africa.

'Khartoum.'

I beat the attaché to it. The buildings became clearer, mosques were discernible but it only added to the ancientness. I recalled history at school and the story of General Gordon and his last stand somewhere down there less than a hundred years before. At a nudge from the attaché I saw the modern control tower of the international airport. Then we were down and into a furnace heat that made me reel in the jet's hatchway a long moment. I was whisked into the VIP lounge where a representative from the ANC office in Khartoum was waiting. He was in a neat Italian suit so he looked like a businessman, except that he was accompanied by a Sudanese in naval uniform. It gave the game away, I thought; with an ANC facility in the Sudan there was probably a corresponding presence of people from the Bureau of State Security, the South African version of the CIA. This part of the airport seemed out of the public gaze though and I was taken to even more restricted surroundings. An identity-tag with my photo and codename in both English and Arabic pinned to my safari jacket, I was jeeped to the airport's military annexe.

Half the Sudanese armed forces seemed to be waiting. Being a logistician I made a quick professional inventory as I passed; there were five T-54 tanks, three Saracen armoured cars, three Vulcan anti-aircraft guns and two SA-2 missile batteries. The uniforms were Eastern-bloc. I knew there was good reason for this state of alertness; the neighbouring international airport, Entebbe in Uganda, had been visited a very short time before by the special forces of not just another country but another continent, those of Israel. South African raiders were every bit as good and it was well known that the two countries with similar under-siege problems had a loose technical alliance at least; they even used the same 'Defence Force' term for their services, as though they were never on the offensive. Entebbe might have given Pretoria ideas. Someone might have planned a long jump even this far to their rear. Every single Frontline state had been hit either by South Africa or the Rhodesian SAS. That was at least my thinking as I was escorted past the bristling weaponry to a Bell 212 helicopter, although, as I later discovered, the Sudanese might have had yet other enemies in mind besides Israelis and Anglo-Boers.

The Bell lifted off from Khartoum and headed east. We came upon massive mountains or *jebels* the colour of treetrunks back home, all bulking out of a burning desert plain. But we were headed for real water, for the Red Sea and Port Sudan, the only place in the country worthy of that prefix. The sea itself mirrored into view with surprisingly scant shipping and I mused at yet another African game-within-a-game. The Suez Canal, not long reopened for the first time since the 1967 Six Day War, had lost out to change in the intervening years. The shipping world had been able to grow in vessel size, being forced to fall back on the older sea route. That route had of course been via the Cape, and the beneficiary had been none other than the government of my South Africa. Almost every move on the continent seemed to bring a countermove. Africa was more than ever the giant chessboard.

The black square of a helipad was waiting for us at Port Sudan naval base. Next to a Yugoslav-built warship lay a Russian freighter which was being unloaded. Its cargo, as I knew perfectly well from an earlier briefing, contained fresh supplies specifically for the ANC, all the way from Odessa on the Black Sea. For various reasons, among them current trouble in the Horn of Africa, it was not running the consignment any further south.

As I stood watching the unloading I looked out to the sea and noticed some half-sunken hulks just offshore. I wondered if these were some of the pathetic ships trapped all those years in the Canal zone who, on their release in 1975, had been of insufficient seaworthiness to complete the voyage to their home port. Beyond, there were distant islands and the coastline of Saudi Arabia. Jedda along that coast was, I knew, a naval base like this one. And there was another city across there which I remembered, thanks to the sudden cessation of the dockside activity around me. Not only the Arab dockers but some of the sailors on guard began to kneel and face across the Red Sea. Holy Mecca was somewhere along that coast too, of course. More Sudanese dropped to pray, and I felt annoyance. One, the unloading of my munitions was being delayed and two, they were breaking a cardinal military rule by letting their guard down. I gave a relieved smile when the unloading began again and a convoy of trucks appeared, as I had expected.

It was when I was actually leaving Port Sudan

at the head of that column, with a last look over my shoulder at the Red Sea, that a not-exactly-warm thought struck me.

Israel, though quite out of sight over that northern horizon, was more a Red Sea presence than ever with its renewed hold on the jutting Sinai peninsula and forward naval bases like Sharm-el-Sheik on the very tip. Had I been an Israeli senior professional, admittedly more to do with intelligence than logistics, I might, with one successful coup under my belt, have made it my business to keep an eye on things down the coast, especially Arab naval bases. From the truck cab I couldn't see them now but they would have been ideal; yes, had I been an IDF officer instead of an ANC one, I would have maintained a special forces' presence of, say, frogmen lying up by day on those rusting offshore hulks.

A man from a hulk—the convict Magwitch—had been the long-term benefactor in that guy Dickens' *Great Expectations*, if you remember; in my case I decided as a young man that I couldn't go on being supported for ever by my Gentleman farmer, so I decided to forego a South African university education. As well as good all-round tuition I had gained a little pride. Though he protested, it was no problem—my Gentleman couldn't be expected to support me along with his own sons, for we had all matriculated. Money had always been a problem in my family, so it was time to return and help them.

In 1951 I returned to Transkei to find a job. Besides my matriculation, I was licensed to drive anything from tractors to heavy goods vehicles. I landed a post in the government, the Department of Agriculture and Forestry. I learnt about trees and timber, hardwood and softwood; Transkei had been heavily deforested over the years but re-planting schemes were under way. Hardly exciting stuff, but I settled down to the work of clearing and log-hauling. Things became even less adventurous when I was promoted to a clerical position.

Life became gentle by 1953. Though there were a few events that year in which I held centre stage, like my marriage to Angelinah Nsongila, there were other happenings of which I was merely a keen observer. There was the Coronation of Queen Elizabeth in London to which I, as a loyal Commonwealth subject, raised a cheer. There was the conquest of Everest which re-awakened my fascination for mountains and made me gaze afresh at the Drakensberg on the northwest horizon. I didn't look much further north then, though I was aware of the changes under way: Kenya and the Mau-Mau, Egypt and the end of King Farouk and then the stirrings in Algeria after the French humiliation at Dienbienphu. But such escalations didn't affect me personally at all; by 1955 I had gone the other way and, as the term goes, had 'got religion'.

In Transkei there had been a mighty crusade by a celebrated African preacher by the name of the Reverend Nicholas Bhengu. The guy could have

been described as a black Billy Graham. I'd gone
to a rally to listen and—pow! To the surprise of my
family—and me—I had a capital 'C' conversion. I
said the words that I accepted Jesus Christ as my
Lord and Saviour in both English and Xhosa.
Within a matter of days my life had completely
changed direction. I gave up my forestry job and
decided to try and become a minister of the church,
which meant going back to school, this time to
Bible school in Pretoria. It was as if the rails had
been switched back and I was a student again, if a
somewhat mature one. In 1957 I emerged with a
diploma in theology and became a probationary
minister in Transkei. A lot of boyhood pals had
trouble believing that Zoleseli Joseph Kobo, the
natural leader in so many games and the usual
winner of so many fights, was now to be found in a
dog collar and was seen walking more in the company of a gentler sort of person. Unlikely people
began to influence me; while other guys talked
excitedly of Jomo Kenyatta and Kwame Nkrumah
and Chief Albert Luthuli, I found a mentor right on
my doorstep.

My mentor was not even a man. This was a
lady with a capital 'L', someone in the same league
as my Bloemfontein Gentleman farmer. Mrs
Sicwetch, her name was, and she was black this
time, but she added immensely to my faith. She
was the powerhouse behind the first church I was
assigned to, a tiny building in an isolated village
called Lujizweni. Mrs Sicwetch had made it more

like a cathedral. This church's congregation would
come from miles around and usually on foot. I
tried to help where I could, getting hold of vehicles and chauffeuring as many as I could. My love
of driving hadn't changed. But, passing my proba-
tion with flying colours with no small thanks to
Mrs Sicwetch and her congregation, my work location was altered. I was assigned, as a full-time
minister, to pastor in towns and cities where
worldliness and radicalness were the rule.

Leaving Port Sudan with my crates aboard a
military convoy, I was reassured to learn that we
would be avoiding any urban areas which might
hold Mossad or BOSS agents and moving straight
into the desert. The weapons and equipment were
of course headed for the far south, but it would
take several days' journey just to reach the
Sudanese border, so I would have sufficient time
for an inspection. I was travelling in the second
vehicle, a Landrover, and was sharing the back seat
with a Sudanese army captain, another Arab, who
looked more like a British officer in his khaki tunic
with its three pips, his peaked cap and Sam
Browne belt. I was still in my safari suit with the
ID tag. The captain's name was Jalloud and he
spoke perfect English, which was probably why he
had been chosen for liaison duties, but I noticed he
emitted a strange hostility towards me. He was a
graduate of Omdurman and Cairo universities, I
had learnt, though I myself kept tight-lipped. I

was still the only negro among them all. For a 'Land of the Blacks', which was the meaning of the word 'Sudan', every soldier seemed to be a tanned Arab.

Captain Jalloud, who wore dark glasses over a hawknose, kept up the conversation, trying to pump me for information.

'Your supply lines, Comrade . . . er . . . Miwe, they must have changed. I mean there's both Somalia and Ethiopia now in civil wars. There's Idi Amin in Uganda who's madder than ever after Entebbe. Do you use Zaire or Kenya? Is it all over-land to a Frontline state or do you fly it on? Why isn't it simply shipped on to Dar-es-Salaam for you, Comrade Miwe?'

I pretended to be asleep with the heat. Jalloud would be handing over command of the convoy to another Sudanese officer well short of the border so he wouldn't know the next stage of this particular supply run and I wasn't about to tell him. I took another look around at the lunar landscape where for years, after slaying General Gordon, the Mahdi had ruled in defiance of British rule in Africa, only to be finally crushed by Kitchener's howitzers. And then ahead, among some black mountains, I saw a sight straight out of that time. We were approaching an army camp with scores of tents. It was Sudanese all right as I saw by a flag, a tricolour pierced by Islamic green.

I was allocated a tent along with Captain Jalloud and then invited to the officers' mess for the evening meal, which I accepted out of politeness. I was dying for a bottle of chilled beer more than anything, but in this part of the world there was no chance. We drank tea, which was perhaps an old British imperial custom and also a reminder of habits back home. I was more keen to see more contemporary influences, namely the Warsaw-Pact consignment in my care.

It was still light when I left the mess and walked to the trucks to identify myself to camp sentries. I did not get a salute, which I put down to my civilian garb. I did however muster the authority to have several random containers opened for a quick inspection. In one I found the folded clothing I was expecting. This was a gift from Czechoslovakia, some suits once used by that country's airborne forces until the pattern had been replaced in the mid-sixties by a more subdued colouring. This old camouflage was very similar to the British-style Dennison used by Boer forces back home, and an advantage for infiltrations. It didn't occur to me, standing in that Sudanese camp, that soon after being issued with their new suits back in the sixties, the Czech military had stood and watched helplessly as the Russians had invaded their country in the so-called 'Prague Spring'. Even had it struck I would have qualified it as a mere hiccup in the world liberation movement. I, like most *Umkhonto* guys, felt nothing but gratitude towards Moscow.

The next crate contained webbing equipment, the belts, pouches and waterbottles to go on those suits. The next held the weapons, the legendary AK-47s, the guns that had won against the West in Asia. There were six carbines in the crate and I picked up one, only to see the Sudanese corporal snap to attention with his SKS rifle by one of the trucks. Captain Jalloud had appeared, having presumably followed me from the mess. He looked down at the opened crates and smiled.

'The mighty Kalashnikov. Shall we have some trials, Comrade Miwe?'

I gave a half-smile, knowing there was no real need. The AKs had been expertly packed back in Europe and they would be thoroughly checked once they had reached a Frontline state. This was just a cursory lookover.

But Jalloud was insistent. 'There is a firing range just outside the camp, Comrade. Surely you have had all the training?'

I had indeed. In at least two Frontline states I had been taught everything about the AK, including stripping and reassembling in jungle darkness. But I was in a safari suit with no need to play soldiers.

'I don't want to break the ammunition box seals, Captain.' I nodded to one of the other trucks. Jalloud whirled and barked an order in Arabic, picking up one of the carbines and pulling out the empty magazine. The corporal pulled opened one of his own pouches and took out a handful of bullets. His SKS was the same calibre as my carbines, I knew. Jalloud gave another shout and two more guards doubled, pulling out spare cartridges.

Jalloud expertly loaded his AK's fibreglass magazine and exchanged it with mine, then armed that weapon. 'Ever noticed the shape of the magazine is Arab?'

I confessed I hadn't as I fell in behind him to our obvious destination, the firing range. The captain seemed determined to have a contest of sorts. The corporal followed but I looked angrily at the trucks and Jalloud ordered the man to stand firm. But other soldiers followed, among them officers. Soon several dozen had left their tents. The range was at the rear of the camp and at the foot of one of the mahogany *jebels.* The targets were Western-style and I thought they had been sited far too close to the rockface, meaning a good chance of ricochets. But Jalloud was adamant. He had now halted with the standard thirty rounds in his magazine and was just under the maximum 400 metres from his target.

'Ten here, ten halfway, ten close range, Comrade. Come on.'

We started forward, his carbine crackling first. I aimed at my target slowly and found myself remembering another teacher besides those Frontline state instructors. I recalled for a moment my Gentleman farmer with his old bolt-action rifles dating from the Great if not the Boer war; and he'd given me one to help him hunt down some wild dogs. I remembered it clear as a bell, on open veldt and us bagging four. Then I remembered where I was, advancing on the target but wary of the sparks and smokevips on the *jebel* rock. I hadn't been trying, but I had an equal score with Jalloud, which wasn't the result he wanted. He turned on his heel, dropped his AK in the dust and marched back to camp followed by the others.

I stayed a moment and looked at the *jebel*. It was not quite a mountain, and there was an out-crop of about three hundred feet. A mad urge came over me. I put down my AK, took off my safari jacket and started up. It was an easy climb and the rock was cooling with the evening. Before I knew it I was up. I had obviously needed to expend something from my system. I looked onto the desert landscape with its weird colouring and then shortened my gaze to the camp. I did a doubletake. It had been laid out with military precision, perhaps from old Empire training. The white tents stretched for a kilometre in ultra-neat rows. I remembered for a moment the 'M' plan Mandela had named after himself back home—the network of cells street by street which no one person would know about, all camouflaged by the ugly misshapen townships. This camp was some-thing like the 'M' plan, as if on a drawing board, but nobody would ever see it like that. I smiled, suddenly not so lonely up there.

I was in fact not on my own at all. Into my line of sight came a sweating, furious face. Jalloud had followed me again. He had seen me climb and had

tried to scale the *jebel* from another slope, but I had
reached the summit first without realising. I gave
a smile to fight the image that occurred to me.
Rolihlahla Mandela was my number-one hero. The
last guy I wanted to identify with was that
blue-eyed general whose last glimpse had been of
murderous Sudanese filling the horizon.

Mandela was the talk of the town in which I
began my full-time ministry; he was the talk of
every urban area in South Africa at the start of the
sixties. Although John Kennedy was the world-
class champ, ennobled with proven military
valour alongside a concern for the oppressed, the
similarly-aged Mandela was the local hero.

Many called him the 'Black Pimpernel', causing
confoundment to the authorities and flitting in and
out of hiding—a will-o'-the-wisp with a silver
tongue and a brilliant legal mind that could out-
articulate all state propaganda.

Then, I smiled at all the adulation. I could
understand why it was so important to have a
flesh-and-blood challenger, especially after the
Sharpeville massacre in which sixty-nine blacks
had been shot dead by government forces. The fact
that I was related to Mandela, that he was a
Transkeian boy made good, gave me some pride.
But pride at that time was a lesser emotion in me,
as was political awareness. The Church was my
calling. I could contribute from that direction,
especially in healing. Sharpeville had surely been

a tragic misunderstanding which the government now regretted.

And yet as I spent more time in towns, or rather black townships outside the proper towns, I became more involved in worldly arguments. Transkeians are well known for thoughtful debate and many political figures come from that area. The ANC, from the word go, drew most of its leadership from this area of the southeast. The geography of the land, while never exactly making the living easy, usually provided time for thought among its men and women, whereas perhaps others in more rugged parts of South Africa had more distraction from the elements. One could draw parallels with the sort of person produced in the English Home Counties and the Scottish Highlands, or New England as opposed to Rocky Mountain folk.

Whatever the reason, Transkei had a history of producing political personalities. Not that we were never fighters—our people were among the first to make contact with the Dutch colonisers in the 1650s and were involved in long-running wars over the centuries with them, long before the Zulus got involved. But debate was in my blood, I suppose, and though a preacher I found my tone getting more worldly. It got increasingly difficult to speak softly in the harshening conditions, with black people having to carry passes and forced to work far from home, as though having been conscripted without dignity or trust. More and more, it seemed there was a battle looming and Transkei itself was becoming that battleground in microcosm, a focus for the whole country.

Something like civil-war feelings had begun to emerge among many locals by 1962, with President Verwoerd, who had already taken us out of the British Commonwealth, deciding to initiate the 'homelands' and getting a fair degree of support among certain blacks. With such 'independence' would come a whole new infrastructure for blacks, with wellpaid jobs in policing, farming and retailing. There would be a new breed of entrepreneurs. Some blacks would do very nicely thank you, especially the politicos. A certain guy by the name of Kaiser Matanzima was one of the chief colluders; some were likening him to a black Marshal Petain. Kaiser and his cronies were out to play Verwoerd's game in order to be a minority elite, like dusky-faced Boers. Blacks as a whole would suffer, though.

Ranged against this view was another Transkeian and the elder statesman of the ANC, Chief Albert Luthuli. Clashes were inevitable. Time and again after church services I would be drawn into the dilemma, hearing worried questions about the future of Transkei. A struggle seemed to be shaping up. Similar struggles had not long finished in Cuba and Algeria and new ones were breaking out in Asia. It seemed that things always ended up militarily and therefore bloodily, unless reason was applied in time.

Perhaps, I thought, sense could be applied before the Transkei problem turned bitter and the white government, seeing their puppets in trouble, turned ugly and intervened. I knew dissenters would be no match in any confrontation; white military firepower would make mincemeat of them. Maybe the government had selected Transkei for their first experiment, thinking the Xhosas were easy meat, gone soft over the years unlike the Zulus to the north. Maybe there was a revenge motive for the help the Xhosas had given to the British during the Boer wars.

Maybe it was with a sense of slight that I, though a clergyman, felt that suddenly in my late twenties my manhood too was being challenged. I slowly got angry. And frustrated. People around me getting caught up in the politics of the moment had still been polite to me, but no more. Maybe they felt I was soft, irrelevant, more like a woman. They were wrong, of course. My dog collar bulged around my neck and I could lift a dozen chairs at any meeting or carry a giant box of Bibles, but it seemed people were looking for a different kind of strength. Maybe I myself felt the same. In any case, after that next year with all those blows, including Mandela's incarceration, I finally removed that dog collar and resigned from the ministry. My preaching skills I kept though, and I was soon speaking at protest meetings, then leading them and then chairing them. The political temperature climbed with me. Verwoerd was trying to sell the homeland packages to the outside world and we were determined there would be no sale.

I got angrier, felt more pressure. I began to change. I started drinking to keep myself going. I took to brandy. South African brandy had a great kick—at least the Huguenots could be thanked for their grape-growing skills. 'Filled with a different kind of spirit now eh, Zoleseli,' one guy remarked over a bottle. I don't think I hit him for the comment, but I put down plenty of people around that time. I'd sometimes go on a crawl, getting drunker and drunker and, just like in films, the bar would go quiet when I entered. With the brandy I put on weight, maybe became a little more appropriately barrel-shaped. There was guilt in me too, I suppose. I'd heard defrocked priests went wild. Anyway, I was trouble. Guys learnt to steer clear of me. I was the kid in the playground with the drover's stick again, ready to spill blood any time. You wouldn't have wanted to meet me on a dark night, even if you'd been able to see me coming.

But with the fear I also got a new respect. Tough guys began to look to me. In the daytime, when I was soon sobered up, I began to make real headway in this new political arena. I joined the Transkei Democrats, the main opposition to Chief Kaiser Matanzima, now that the ANC and Pan-African Congress were banned. In many ways though, this was old wine in new bottles, the same people agitating. It was an umbrella organisation and ANC expertise, advice and funding became

available. Matanzima's arch rival Chief Luthuli
played the game well, sidestepping the traps that
had landed the younger lions like Mandela in
prison. I learnt and got into a faster stride. Other
events in southern Africa such as Ian Smith declar-
ing UDI or Verwoerd keeping hold of Namibia
were just grist to the mill. The political animal in
me got wilder, and as I met more and more
committed people the radical germ passed into me
and took over. By 1966, I was passing out the literature of not only Mandela but Mao and Guevara,
where once I had dealt in hymnsheets and Bibles.

But as well as political headway, I was also
making enemies by the score.

I now knew that the Sudanese captain, despite
his country's support for the ANC, was a hostile
force. He continued to call me 'comrade', though.
We left the *jebel* camp and headed south on the
next stage of the supply trail to a Frontline state.
Again he kept probing about eventual routes and
again I feigned sleepiness. My eyes kept opening
though at the changing terrain. We were slowly
leaving the Sahara and dropping into a more familiar Africa. Yellow sand-glare became brownness
and then near-greenery. Trees with real foliage
were taking over from the date palms and there
was less a sense of the nomadic, though we were
still north of the White Nile.

The ground beneath our tyres was more solid
now and the convoy was bouncing where before it

had sailed. I had started to worry about the crates
when there was a cough.

'Comrade Miwe. We have a "frontline" state of
sorts. This province we're entering.'

The desert road had become a dirt track and we
saw, ahead, a stone building flying the Sudanese
tricolour. The building was a tan-coloured fort dating from colonial times and it was garrisoned by a
full company. Some of the soldiers here, I noticed,
were darker-skinned, though not negroid.

Captain Jalloud nodded as some of these soldiers joined the turnout of the guard. 'You were
never of the Muslim faith though, Comrade
Miwe?' He turned to me for an instant and, knowing I would not answer, nodded to several Nubians
presenting arms. 'Neither are they.'

Jalloud, I realised, was referring to Sudan's
internal problem, the ancient hostility between the
Arabic and Muslim north and the black south who
were either animist or Christian in religion. A
fierce civil war had raged well into the seventies,
until President Numeiri had announced a
'Southern Solution'. Taking in the M-13 Walid carriers corralled in the fort, I wondered if he had only
achieved a lull.

The fort was to be our next halt, but Captain
Jalloud had no intention of resting. After a scratch
lunch of stew which could have been camel, he
appeared with two corporals in tow. I saw they
were carrying a weapon between them. It was an
RPG-7 rocketlauncher with a pack of reloads, all

Warsaw-Pact issue. It was nominally an anti-tank weapon, but could come in useful in house clearing.

'I don't know if you have any of these in your consignment. Or any SAM-7s.'

Again I didn't say much. I was dying for some coffee, having developed a taste for the Arab variety. He waited for an answer, so I shrugged.

'We do carry rockets occasionally, Captain. But it's mainly bush, thicker than this, our area of operations. The AK is our mainstay, light and fast-firing as it is. Heavy machine-guns and mortars would slow you down more than anything.'

'But the RPG is man-portable. *Imshi.*' Jalloud ordered the NCOs to equip him with the launcher, the pack strapped to his back. He handed his cap to one and smiled to his Landrover. 'Some more firing practice, comrade.'

I shrugged again. Another challenge, another duel of sorts. He used English as before, but this time several of the dusky soldiers nearby, including an officer, seemed to understand. Jalloud realised this the next moment and glared over. The dark soldier, one pip on each collar, looked defiant. I wondered if in this fort were rumblings of mutiny between Arab and non-Arab Sudanese. I also wondered if my defiance of Jalloud might encourage anything ugly and decided to placate.

'I have fired RPG, Captain.'

Jalloud grinned. 'Fine. Three HEAT rounds in this pack. One each and one to the winner. Not in here of course.'

The firing was to be done outside the fort. It was about two miles in the Landrover, with two Walids escorting us. We drove through a village, a ghost village that was more like a bombsite, and I noticed the Walid crews start to scan the flanking undergrowth with wide eyes. I wondered if there were anti-government elements in the area, or if fighting had spilled over the Ethiopian border.

Jalloud grunted and our driver braked. Ahead stood a blockhouse shape. It was similar to the army fort, but its stone a deeper red. There were holes in it, shellholes. Its shape resembled a pyramid, though it was too small and this was too far down the Nile. I realised this was the target. Jalloud unslid a HEAT round from the pack himself and looked irritably at his driver who came forward and loaded him. Feet planted firmly, the soldier smacking his shoulder, Jalloud elevated the RPG at the pyramid. 'The very tip, Comrade Miwe'.

I realised that the sun, less the furnace here, was setting over the target and Jalloud had positioned himself to fire into the west. A hit would tear off some of the tip and make a second sunrise. It was all very poetic, but I could have done without any of it. Cradling the RPG, Jalloud nodded. I waved a soldier back from his immediate rear. Jalloud fired and we watched the projectile soar into the air as the sun touched the pyramid. There was a blast and a sear of sun, but too low. Jalloud had hit the structure, but just below the tip.

He snarled and turned to me.

'I'll load you, Comrade.'

The 'OK' on my shoulder was like a rabbit punch a few seconds later. I squinted through the sight and was blinded by sun. It was difficult but I had been trained in adverse conditions back in my Zambian base. As instructors had intoned, if the balloon ever really went up back home and it was open warfare, we would need to storm Boer barracks, police stations and armouries and RPGs would be the quickest, cleanest door-openers. I squeezed, the rocket flew right at the tip and clipped the lefthand side, revealing more of the sunset. There came a quiet grunt from some watching soldier, a sound that quickly faded. Jalloud glared from the grunt to me and gave that scimitar-smile again.

'Bravo again, comrade. The final round is yours. Right centre and the whole tip will go.'

I launched the last rocket and it missed completely as I'd intended, to return some face to Jalloud before his men. But there was no grace on him whatever as I handed the launcher over.

'Accidental near-miss, comrade . . . surely a *church* does not bother you?'

It vaguely registered that my target had once been a place of worship for Sudan's beaten Christian south, but the Captain was correct. I was busily looking forward to a new liaison man and a new stage of my arms run south. For the problems of that country, whether desertification or desecration, I frankly didn't give a damn.

4

The Town Prison

Name	KOBO
Christian name	JOSEPH
Clan name	ZOLESELI
Height	5' 9"
Weight	12 stone
Race	Bantu/Xhosa

*B*y early 1966 my description must have started appearing on police files at Transkei police headquarters in Umtata, with copies forwarded to their white puppetmasters in Pretoria. After over two years travelling throughout the homeland and beyond, visiting major cities and making ever widening contacts with the Transkei Democrats and the ANC, I would have received classification as a troublemaker, loudmouth, public enemy and possible Communist. For such persons new laws had been invented. This was called the Suppression of Communism Act and in Transkei, Proclamation R400. Even at all the dozens of public meetings throughout Transkei with not a uniform in sight, there would have been plenty of police informers, once in a while holding a hidden camera. I wasn't a Communist, in fact, and had no intention of joining that party with its inherent belief in rule by the working class, though I had moved far closer to the ANC, but to the Boers anyone doing what I was doing was without the shred of a doubt in up to his neck with Moscow. That year there was more fuel added to such beliefs; South Africa had its own presidential assassination when Dr Verwoerd died after being stabbed on a podium. Although his killer was a white, it only added to the supremacists' paranoia.

I should have been prepared for it. I was in my family home outside Umtata. I now had Thandi and Sadile, a son and a daughter, the typical nuclear family. The police exploded on my house one night like a bomb. The house was surrounded, the front door booted in, my kids were awoken in terror by gutteral shouts and barking Alsatians and I was slammed half-dressed into a Maria—black of course. I was taken to the central police station in Umtata, charged under Proclamation R400 and given a 90-day detention, without trial. It could have been worse; the year before the police had doubled the span for real troublemakers. Ninety days, though, is three solid months and for someone who'd never been in trouble—the beerhall fights were never reported—it was traumatic enough.

I got a reminder of those fights very quickly, though this time I didn't win, because I didn't hit back. When it first happened, when those three black cops came at me in the interrogation cell and used their fists and sticks, I used my head. I could have actually taken all three, could have butted them out one by one, but I would have gained nothing except three, six, more of them and in their fury they would have crippled me and put me out of the game for good. The Transkei police grilled me, tried to catch me out but I couldn't help them much. For a start, I wasn't the rabid red of their dreams and couldn't give much information about the Communist party, nor had I met its leader Joe Slovo. I hadn't been to Russia—I hadn't at that time ever been abroad.

I was sorry but my help to their enquiries was extremely limited. I was sworn at, mainly in Xhosa. Three more of Umtata's finest closed in with piledrivers and uppercuts. This second time it occurred to me that my beerhall opponents had been much tougher. Those ones had been manual workers with hard-muscled power who could hurt. My taunters were the worst of soft Transkeians, puppet-types who hardly bothered with gym workouts. It occurred to me that they weren't really hurting. As I said before, my build comes close to a tank or barrel so I could take a lot of punishment. Especially if I knew that wrong wasn't entirely on my side.

I remember a particular moment during that

79

second beating in the middle of the night at Umtata, though. One sergeant's punch actually hurt badly, to the point where I was just about stung into instant retaliation and might have broken his neck. Just as I was about to cascade I suddenly found myself talking calmly to my companions.

'Is that,' I asked of my main tormentor, 'the only punch you can do? You beat like—'

'Like what?' the man, a sergeant asked, sensing grudging respect.

'Like your wife.' I replied.

'What did you say, Kobo?'

'I think you heard.'

'You–'

'Look, sergeant. If this is all you can do you're wasting your time. The way you're panting, you and these boys, shows you're getting tired. It's late. Anyway, speaking of your wife, why not go home to her?'

'Kobo, Kobo, Kobo–'

'I hear you. Look, by all means keep hitting me but I can't tell you anything. I'm not a Communist. Sure I'm against Chief Kaiser, but I'm not able to give you info, any info at all. So you're welcome to go on punchbagging but I don't see the point. What do you think, sergeant?'

'Kobo. Kobo, I'll–'

'Sarge,' one of the constables broke in, still panting from all his swinging. 'Leave the Commie. We'll be off-duty in an hour. Let him stew here.'

Thus that second interrogation ended. But there were more. There were always more police of differing characters. Some never used fists, some used boots. Some were technocrats. They would attach their gleaming electrics to your private parts. You would scream, and scream. But again, you couldn't help. There would be the hangmen, who would stand you on a chair in a noose, hands behind your back, for hours, knowing you daren't fall asleep because you'd be off the chair and in space, for ever. The official report would say suicide. I once stood on such a scaffold for two whole days, unmoving. For some, it was quicker by tube. Guards would have a tyre's inner tube which they would slit open and place over your head as a suffocation bag. You would struggle and lose consciousness and they'd revive you just in time. Having sown such terror in you, they'd appear with another inner tube a few weeks later. Again I went out, came round, but couldn't tell them anything. Then there were those guards with an agricultural bent. A large mealie or maize bag ...

In that guy Dumas' *Count of Monte Cristo* they put the hero in a sack, if you remember, and put the sack into the sea, making it possible to effect an underwater escape. They put me into this mealie bag and put me into deep water—it could have been seawater because it was apparently the Umtata estuary where it flows into the Indian Ocean. I went underwater but I didn't escape. The bag was held fast by a mechanical crane, though

I'd have preferred the feathered version. It sub-
merged me till I thought I was drowning and then
hoisted me into the air. The water was freezing; it
also contracted the bag like a vice. I hung in the
air, those guys freezing me and squeezing me. The
crane swung me to the bank where they hit the bag
with sticks. It was a memorable night, but I still
had nothing to tell them beyond the fact that I
politically opposed Chief Kaiser.

I got moved from Umtata. Perhaps pressure
had come from higher up and cleverer questioning
was required. I was taken from Transkei which, if
Pretoria was playing the game, would have been
illegal as it was after all a self-governing 'homeland'.

I arrived at Port Elizabeth *'Maksimium'* prison
and had white faces around me. A new game now
developed—duelling with Boers. They were of
course no alien race to me, thanks to my
Gentleman farmer of the forties. I had lived
among them day and night. I knew how a lot of
them ticked.

A lot of them, the Afrikaners, are more like us
than the Anglo-Saxon whites. They have simply
lived here longer—more of them have walked the
land. I knew, to pursue the clock analogy, that you
could, if you were intelligent, stop them ticking for
a while by switching them off. In broad generalisa-
tion, the Boer can be fierce and cruel, but he is a
straight man of his word and he can laugh. I
decided to switch them off with laughter and,

speaking generally again, it worked—in Port
Elizabeth anyway. I'd remember so many of my
younger days and know what to say to deflect
verbal slings and arrows. A red face with the look
of a wild pig would suddenly break into a grin and
mutter 'You cheeky kaffir' and the interrogation
would be over for the evening.

Then, of course, the pig-look would harden
into that of a rhino with a skin you couldn't get
through. Then it would be physical and he'd
teach you manners for such cheek. That was more
the way of things in Durban. There, you'd meet
men that made you wonder why the Boers hadn't
joined Hitler instead of the Allied side, though of
course in 1939 there were many who would certainly have jumped Germany's way, given the
chance. Himmler would have wept with admiration at the interrogation techniques; I wept on my
own, with pain and rage. My face ballooned from
swelling. Marlon Brando would have wept with
admiration. But still I couldn't tell even these
Boers much, except I was against all Chief Kaiser
Matanzima stood for.

And then the blows to the face suddenly
stopped, then those to my stomach. I realised I
was being made ready to face the outside world
with no telltale signs. Sure enough, on a December
day in '66, with the country calmer now that a guy
called Vorster had successfully taken the reins from
Verwoerd, I was returned to Transkei. A doctor
had checked me and there was no bruising. I was

Sidney-Poitier-handsome again and I thought the
90-day thing was really no big deal, because after
all Mandela had now done three times 365 days on
that island down by the Cape. I at least had my
liberty but I was a marked man, I knew. I'd had a
warning and no matter where I went in South
Africa, if I was caught stirring up more trouble it
would be much, much worse next time. A lot of
people, friends and enemies, knew that. It was
quite a dilemma, knowing your every move would
be watched, but there was one simple solution
which Mandela in the same situation had effected.
It would also have made that dame—no, she
ranked higher than a dame—OK, that Baroness
Orczy weep with admiration. This was to simply
Pimpernel myself out of South Africa.

5

Tanzania

*T*he sixties film *Zulu* was the most famous South Africa-based picture ever released and when, a decade later, they came to make the sequel they imported a real Hollywood star for maximum box-office appeal. That guy Burt Lancaster, though he was more a veteran of cavalry versus Indian Westerns, was cast as a British army officer and as 'Zulu Dawn' told the story of the impis' victory at Isandlwana in which the redcoats were wiped out to a man, and he too had to fall. Except that being Burt Lancaster, he wasn't taken out by a Zulu . . . but by an Apache adviser attached to the Zulus.

It was never a great joke to me either but as far as southern Africa was concerned there was a ring of serious truth. Old adversaries from far afield would make their appearance. On the one hand there might be British or Americans who had lately joined the Rhodesian forces, and on the other Russians or East Germans would buttress the black guerrillas. South African soldiers would also have 'volunteered' to join in the duelling and, though

ANC were largely under training, we would sometimes be called upon to support actions. Taking it a
notch up, when white special forces launched
attacks into Frontline states, men from the same
part of South Africa would sometimes find themselves facing one another.

Of those Frontline states, the first to be established and the most remote was Tanzania—and yet
that was where I witnessed one or two weird incidents . . .

Tanzania had achieved its independence in the
very early '60s from Britain, who had taken it from
the Germans in World War One when it was
known as Tanganyika and Zanzibar. The new
President Julius Nyerere—'the Teacher' to
Africans—had immediately offered help to nearby
nationalists such as FRELIMO, ZANLA and the
Military Wing of the ANC. It was in a Tanzanian
clearing that Nelson Mandela had briefed the very
first *Umkhonto* cadre; they had gone on north for
training while he turned south, to capture and
Robben Island. But more and more cadres had
come to Tanzania as the sixties grew into the seventies, and among the intakes was me.

My cadre had entered the southeastern border
region for training by foreign instructors. The men
we met were, even for me, disconcerting at first
glance. They were a pair, an officer and sergeant
seconded from East German special forces, and
they seemed not unfamiliar. Their looks, manner-
isms and gutteral accents reminded us of the

quintessential Afrikaner. For the ZIPRA men in our cadre it was probably different, for their direct opponents in Rhodesia were closer to Australians in many ways.

For a few of *my* guys though, it was difficult to believe that the men ordering us about were not of the same ilk as the uniformed Boer we knew so well. In fact these ones were even more like classic Nazis. As one of our political officer-commissars, if you will, pointed out, however, these were very different Germans, practising Marxist ideology. They were, I learnt, both Berliners, and it was sobering to think they represented a carved-up city which had in 1878 been the host to a Treaty conference which had carved up Africa. Our instructors must have had a few reminders of old imperial Germany in Tanzania, but they didn't say much at first. Oh, they were good. The Russians had selected Honecker's forces out of all their satellites for African secondment; I recalled reading that Lenin himself had once said Germans were better potential Communist cadres than even his own countrymen. Though I myself had received previous training, we were put through our paces. To be hit-and-run men required fitness. None of us, though, were weaklings, thanks to labouring days back home. Some had worked in the Rand gold-fields or the Witbank steelmills, and most of us were angry young men who had been in at least one brawl.

After several weeks we could appreciate the

instruction, though some of the guys were still resentful. Me, I made it my business to get on with all sorts, and in fact I was a keen supporter when the *Stabsgefreiter* made an advenurous suggestion, as we were all quartered in Tanzania. The country contains Africa's highest peak, Mount Kilimanjaro, which was first climbed by a German during imperial days. Our instructors probably betrayed a latent nationalism in their idea of trying the ascent themselves. It was a five-day climb and it could be part of our training.

I was first to support the idea, still having that fascination for mountains since the days I'd gazed at the Drakensberg when a kid. Permission was sought through commissars and the Tanzanian authorities. The notion unwound the instructors further. One Tanzanian product we had all taken to was coffee and we'd drink gallons of the stuff together around campfires. The lieutenant was a keen Communist who had taken part in the 1968 crushing of Czechoslovakia, when only trusted GDR troops had been allowed to go in with the Russians. I made no comment. My interest was seventies Africa, not sixties Europe. They talked more. Their real hate was for their fellow-Germans in the West whom they regarded as soft. Whether the outlook was based on genuine spartanism or simple jealousy I never discovered.

I trained with them in some high country for another week, only to find out that the climb had been vetoed by the Nyerere government. There

were apparently too many tourists in the country
and Kilimanjaro's slopes were too public. The
instructors were allowed to go, however. They left
our camp one morning, changed into safari suits
but looking far more martial than us in our camouflage, and we never saw them again. They were
found dead on Kilimanjaro a week later, having
apparently fallen. Both had been trained paratroopers. One of my cadre suggested that maybe
they had tried a jump off the mountain, or been
pushed. Others grinned, more taken with a cheap
racial joke than a more sinister explanation.

And the issue of race had been given an extra
tilt in Tanzania. A new colour was present in con-
siderable numbers, here alone of all the Frontline
states. Nyerere, to the consternation of the usual
Cold-War players, had invited in Red China. 'The
Teacher' had taken up Peking's offer of assistance
for his great dream, a railway running down to
Zambia. The Russians and the West, having decided the project was uneconomical, had refused
cash and both had watched open-mouthed as
China had poured in men and machinery, with the
'Tanzam' or 'Freedom Line' opening in 1975. The
line had been a cut across other people's mainsails
and Chinese influence was still very present, not
only with rail experts but military instructors who
by now outnumbered East Germans and Russians.
As far as Nyerere was concerned, Oriental contact
was nothing new. There had been links between
his coast and the Far East since Manchu times. But

for nearby countries, both black and white, the presence of so many Chinese was a highly unsettling factor.

I had no Chinese instruction during any of my five tours in Tanzania. I was there largely for logistical purposes, helping move supplies south and making great use of the Tanzam, which was also known as the 'Bamboo Line'. Trains would bring arms shipments unloaded at Dar-es-Salaam to our main camp at Morogoro, whence it would be despatched down to bases in Zambia.

On one such night I was at a small station a few stops on from Morogoro, awaiting a new supply train. It was a calm clear night and I was in camouflage suit with my ID tag. I had my waterbottle filled with local coffee to keep me going. The station was deserted, but for a few Tanzanian soldiers who had challenged me and then wandered off. The train was late and I had gathered that preference was being given to tank trains headed north for their troubled Ugandan border, where the rogue-elephant regime of Idi Amin was doing more damage to black nationalism than the entire Pretoria government. I waited patiently for my train. After a while I heard a faint roar out of the jungle and saw a motorcyclist halted on the far side of the track. I noticed he was not African but Chinese. He was in the usual drab uniform and Mao cap which was slightly windblown from the riding. There was a large pannier on the back. I was only slightly curious. Maybe he was a

maintenance man, keeping a weather eye on
stretches of the Tanzam, I thought. He noticed me
on the station. He then bent to his machine. I
wondered if the engine was giving him trouble. I
checked there was no sign of the Dar-es-Salaam
train and started across the line. On my
Gentleman farmer's place as a youth I had tinkered
with two-stroke engines, so maybe I could help.
His Bamboo Line was helping us enough. But at
my approach the Chinese looked up in some alarm
and began fidgeting frantically with his starter. I
noticed his machine was Japanese, a world away
from a 1940s BSA, but maybe there was a simple
problem.

'*Jambo*,' I called in Swahili as I approached,
about the only word I knew. There was no reaction. He could see I was military, probably took
me for a Tanzanian soldier, but he seemed nervous.

Knowing no Chinese, I tried English.
'Comrade, can I be of help?' His cap went closer
to his engine as though hiding his face. I noticed
something taped to his pannier. It looked like a
black-painted knife. Maybe he had no proper
tools. I patted my waterbottle.

'Coffee, comrade. Like some coffee?'
He said something then. It sounded as if he was
repeating my words. Then I saw his face turn
wolfish. He looked at his pannier and then we
both heard the unmistakable swish of a locomo-
tive. Suddenly the motorcycle started up, sweet as
a bird without so much as a cough. The Chinese

pulled his cap down hard and swung right round, making me reel out of the way, and then he was gone back into the jungle, and the motorcycle's roar was being replaced by the train. It was my train. I boarded it as planned, liaising with a Tanzanian officer and soon we were crossing the Zambian border for our main supply base at Mbala.

It was some time later in that base that the curious footnote came. A political officer-commissar, if you will, briefed us about new enemy activity. The opposition had some more tricks. White special forces had been turning up in various Frontline states in the guise of East German, Cuban or Russian instructors. The culprits were probably SAS or Selous Scouts. I nodded. Good behind-the-lines specialists should be doing just that anyway. OK, so we would be all on our guard.

I woke up later that same night in my tent and it clicked. I wondered if I had heard right, because I was certain that the man in the Mao cap outside Morogoro hadn't gruffly repeated the word 'coffee' at all but had said in a not-unfamiliar accent the familiar term 'kaffir'.

It was just possible that my motorcyclist had not been that far from home. Maybe, instead of the mysterious East, he had simply come from East London, or Port Elizabeth, or Cape Town, all of which have minorities of Chinese who had arrived to work the Rand goldfields during the days of Empire and stayed on to be classified as

'Coloureds', yet who were still eligible for service in the armed forces. Perhaps I had it all wrong, but maybe some smart-alec of a special forces' commander had inserted exactly the right sort of man for a nose or a spot of sabotage on the Bamboo Line and my appearance had thrown things. Maybe that knife taped to his pannier had been a Boer-made Warlock and it would have gone into my jugular, had not the Tanzam train just sounded.

Or maybe it had all been harmless. I lay back on my groundsheet and stayed awake for a while, hearing the wind sigh in the overhead camphor trees. Or maybe it was me.

6

The Tower of London

*T*he elusive Sir Percy Blakeney and I had even
more in common; for our bolthole from a land in
political turmoil both of us Pimpernels had chosen
exactly the same city, London.

It had not actually been my idea; rather it was
at the behest of old friends in England, pen-pals I
had made during my time as a pastor. They had
often put the suggestion that I should complete my
studies and give myself a breath of fresh air by taking up an overseas scholarship. Now, appalled on
learning of my 90-day detention without trial, they
had pulled strings. There was the offer of a course
in theology should I want to come to their neck of
the woods. The only thing was, I was no longer a
genuine theologian. I nonetheless considered the
offer and consulted fellow-radicals. Everyone saw
it as an ideal opportunity to slip out of the lime-
light, let the heat cool and maybe attain more education for the cause. Not a few guys were envious
of another break that had come for me, through
white guys of all people. Bachelor of Divinity was

the sort of target my English friends had in mind
for me, and when I accepted their proposal, wheels
were set in motion. I said goodbye to my family in
the usual stoic African way and made my first
traumatic move, slipping up into a Frontline state
and its international airport. Local ANC were also
helping and would provide me with my passport,
courtesy of the United Nations.

The country I slipped into was of course
Botswana—this was the very first occasion—and
soon I was airborne for the very first time, tran-
scending even my Drakensberg mountains. The
out-of-Africa route was similar to the one Mandela
had taken after training and lobbying in Saharan
countries; in London he had met the British opposition leaders Gaitskell and Grimond, though not
the Conservative Prime Minister Macmillan, even
though the latter had been the architect of the
African 'Wind of Change'. I had been with enough
ANC people to have learnt of Mandela's mixed
emotions concerning Britain, a place that was the
very heart of an old empire that had ruled so many
non-white people and yet a place of warm familiarity.

I knew my British history better than most
black guys, and probably many whites. I remembered dates and aligned them with my own country even as I was arriving. There appeared the
English Channel and the straits where the Spanish
Armada had foundered under storm and fireships,
whereby the Protestants had taken the ascendancy
in seafaring, which had brought the Dutch and

British to, among other places, the southern tip of Africa.

I landed in a grey Heathrow and shivered with the cold. The friends waiting to greet me had dismal news; I would be unable to study Divinity as I did not have any learning in Hebrew. But there were still avenues open and I could switch to another subject.

To cut a long story short, I decided to plump for something much more worldly, namely the subject of economics. I was accepted by the London School of Economics, which by 1967 had already become notorious as a place of student unrest. European youth was developing a conscience about its countries' colonial pasts. Though British students were very aware of the situation in South Africa they were more concerned with Biafra, and even more so with Vietnam. Protest marches, sit-ins and huge rallies were becoming the norm for most LSE people, but not for me. From the word go I kept my head down. I had a duty to people back home to educate myself for their benefit, and such international awareness, though very noble, seemed a distraction more than anything.

I made friends with many students though, but naturally was drawn towards fellow Africans, especially South Africans. One such guy came from Natal and was an Indian. 'Ram'—as I'll call him—was much more politically developed than me. His idol was Gandhi, who had once walked on Natal soil. Ram had a worrying theory.

Though thousands of miles from home, he thought he was still under observation. Ram was convinced non-white South Africans undergoing political education abroad were being monitored, even guys like us. It seemed a lot to swallow. I wondered if he should have been studying psychology rather than economics, perhaps majoring in paranoia.

I knew of course that because the ANC hierarchy was based in London with Oliver Tambo, the next-most-important figure after Mandela, there must also be a BOSS presence. Their London operation was little reported by the British press except for papers like the *Guardian*. It was obvious that BOSS was based in South Africa House, only a mile or so away from the LSE, at the end of the Strand by Trafalgar Square, and there was a joke concerning the feelings of the staff at being permanently overlooked in that location by a guy called Nelson. But surely jokes were the limit. I realised BOSS would be watching some ANC exiles but their main job here would be counterpropaganda or disinformation to the British public, especially with the Wilson administration having banned arms sales to Pretoria in 1966. Surely they would never bother with small fry like me.

Yet my friend Ram was convinced. Despite the arms ban, he reminded me, there were continuing military links between the British and South African forces, such as the shared use of the giant Simonstown naval base on the Cape. I shook my head. As well as the era of 'Swinging London' it was also the time of fanciful spy stories from Ian Fleming and Len Deighton.

And then, as if to throw me, I heard news from back home, of the mysterious death of Chief Luthuli, the leader of the Transkeian opposition. Out walking on a route he knew like the back of his hand, he had been hit by a train. It was terrible, but it was back home. This was carefree London. There was television, an eyeopener to me coming from a country that only had a radio service, but I found myself avidly watching that series 'The Prisoner' with its paranoia-at-every-turn atmosphere. The scenes where the hero was chased and smothered by a weird animated bubble made me remember the warders with their inner-tube game. But I buried my head in study, bookworming most of my course. Some students were hardly ever indoors; they were too busy being angry at the outside world.

The Tet offensive in Vietnam momentarily caught my attention; people who throughout history had been a subject race were actually surprising the mightiest Anglo-Saxons in the world . . . but I soon had my head down again. The early months of 1968 were freezing and my African blood suffered. I sometimes felt like screaming at the excitable comings and goings because they brought open doors and draughts. Then I put down my books for a while as the months got warmer but news got icier. Senator Robert Kennedy had been gunned down like his brother.

Another white with concern for blacks, a man who had actually gone to South Africa and met with Chief Luthuli, 'Bobby' was no longer able to help. And then the bullets found Martin Luther King. I cried on both those days.

But I was not in violent America but friendly England where I had the freedom to study. There were still wrongs even here though, and the more I studied the history of economics the more I learnt about corruption and greed as unchanging entities. LSE, as someone pointed out, also stood for Living Streets of Exploitation. But I now loved those streets. I did a lot of walking after studies. It was still the 'swinging' era, the time of Love and Tolerance. Blacks had largely only been in Britain a decade or so and the ones born domestically were still kids, not yet a problem to police. There was some discrimination, though, with West End clubs and discotheques blaring soul music but barring black guys at the door. But this was a world better than back home.

There was familar history on nearly every street corner. Right by the LSE there was a little shop which was none other than the Old Curiosity Shop that that guy Dickens had named a novel after. You could make so many connections with South Africa, too; not far away were the Houses of Parliament, which not only Mandela had visited at the start of the decade but which the original ANC leadership humbly entered in 1912 to protest about the Boers' Land Act, a problem swiftly eclipsed by

the start of the Great War. There was Petty France
nearby, named after the Huguenots who had come
to London in one of the two main exoduses by
those French Protestants, the other exodus being to
the Cape where they had formed the second wave
of whites. Funnily or unfunnily enough it was
between both those London locations, in Victoria
Street, that I one day remembered that paranoiac
warning from my fellow student, Ram.

A man appeared to be following me. He was
white, middle-aged and in a raincoat. I went into a
record shop, attracted by some classical music,
came out and he was waiting. He kept about a
hundred yards behind. I crossed the street and he
did likewise. At any one time in a city street there
are probably a thousand people walking together
and I tried to forget him. He was still there ten
minutes later. Ram's paranoia touched me. Less
than a hundred people knew of my presence in
London. But could my UN passport have been
scrutinised by British Special Branch at Heathrow
and details passed to BOSS? It was possible,
Labour government or not. I walked to Marble
Arch and the man was still the hundred yards
behind. He could be, I had decided, a pickpocket
or a weirdo or a policeman. And if not a white South
African, he had certainly become a bore. Confront-
ing him and maybe starting a fight might get me
into trouble and deportation, I decided, and leapt
onto a doubledecker bus at Piccadilly and lost him.

Or I had for the moment. If he was BOSS and

knew about me he'd simply stake out the LSE building. I mentioned it to Ram after a lecture there the next day. He nodded and gave me more advice, this time to watch out for followers who were not on foot—drivers, he said. Being at the wheel of a vehicle meant a perfect excuse for mobility; even Mandela himself had posed as a chauffeur during his Pimpernel days back home. Taxis, Ram added. London taxis were the perfect cover for opposition agents. Taxis were in every street, and they all looked the same.

Except, I put in, one thing about hackney carriages made them unlikely BOSS vehicles . . . they were all black.

Ram did not laugh, and neither did I some weeks later. Another LSE student—a Kenyan— and I decided to visit the Tower of London. With next to no money, we walked up through the City to Tower Hill and, glancing behind, I saw a slow-moving London taxi with a male passenger. He was in casual shirt with a neckslung camera, but it looked like the guy from Victoria.

My Kenyan companion was totally unaware of any problem and I kept it that way. We entered the Tower complex and gaped at the ancient battlements and above them a wheeling raven. The Kenyan consulted his guidebook, but I knew so much off by heart from schooldays and stopped looking literally behind me. I was now in the fortress built by William, the Norman who was more tellingly a Viking. We climbed the stairs where they had found the bodies of the two Princes supposedly murdered by the Crookback King and we saw the area where a condemned noblewoman had lost her composure and fled from the execution block, only to be pursued by the headsman and hacked piecemeal on the run. There were the Crown Jewels and there was the all-but-forgotten Traitor's Gate by the river, where prisoners made their watery approach. Then we met another group of black tourists who turned out to be Kenyan. Realising my companion would be some time and wanting to return for more studying, I left the Tower alone and headed back west.

I was one street away when I noticed a slow-moving taxi following. I waved him away thinking he was looking for a fare. But it halted and I glimpsed a passenger already aboard. I also spotted a neckslung camera. I moved quickly into a sidestreet and then an alley and found myself alone again. I looked up and found I was by the Monument, the column to the Great Fire of London started in a baker's shop, and where at least three bakers have made death-leaps. I also remembered that forties film in which a foreign correspondent, pursued by fascist agents operating in London, had narrowly missed being hurled off that same 200-foot high Monument. I gave the column a wide berth and headed north.

This time two taxis appeared, but whole families were in the back complete with cameras. I smiled. Of course this highly historic area would be full of picture-takers. I would never be sure if the man outside the Tower had been really familiar anyway. Still smiling, I continued up Gracechurch Street and found myself wandering into St Michael's Place. More history was here in the form of a plaque. I was standing on the site of London's very first coffee-house called the 'Pasquale Rose'. It reminded me how thirsty I was, and how good a strong cup would taste. A modern coffee-bar wouldn't be far away. Then I noticed the date on the plaque. It was a year long burned into my head. It was 1652.

At precisely the same time as this peaceful London shopowner was first brewing his coffee, the Boers were landing on the Cape and encountering my forebears. It meant nothing of course but I forgot about drinking from a cup and waited till the nearest pub opened and, though I could ill-afford it, ordered a double brandy.

I never saw anyone resembling that camera-man again. In '68 I graduated from the LSE as a Bachelor of Science. I never saw Ram again. He probably remained in Britain and became more activist, or maybe he changed completely and settled down to a married middle-class life. I returned to South Africa after nearly two years' absence, with many fond memories, though by then I'd forgotten all about that afternoon by the Tower. I had no idea that within a few months I would be being boated in through what many thought of as the modern, properly guarded Traitor's Gate.

7

The Island Prison

*R*obben Island, or *Robbeneiland* in Afrikaans, is one of the very few sea-surrounded spots in the Cape region, or indeed the whole of the RSA. The even smaller Dassen Island lies nearby and there is Ladies' Rock just to the north but not much else. The currents of both the Atlantic and Indian oceans are just too strong, culminating as they do in the 'Wild' and 'Skeleton' coasts with the shipwrecks that lie in their thousands. South Africans, both black and white, are therefore unfamilar with the lure and lore of islands, though for the former by the seventies the word *esiquithini*—'on the rock'—meant just one thing, the offshore cage holding Mandela and his hundred other colleagues. A few uneven square miles of scrub-covered limestone, the island had first been used as a prison by the first Dutch of the 1652 landings. A black named Herri had rebelled against the whites' leader Van Riebeek and had been cast onto the rock. Herri had been a Khoi-Khoi or Hottentot, but the next prisoner had been Xhosa. And the next and the

next. Even more of that tribe had found themselves on Robben as, over the next century, war
after war had been waged on the Boers. There
came the founding of a Leper colony, though political prisoners also arrived right through Victorian
times. Then the World Wars had thundered,
enhancing the importance of the Cape route to the
Allies. Robben had been turned into a fortress
along Gibraltarian lines, with a similar network of
tunnelled artillery. The batteries had never been
put to the test, for after the *Graf Spee* scuttling the
Germans had largely ceased surface operations in
the South Atlantic. With 1945 the noble comparisons with Gibraltar and Corregidor ended, though
it remained a military establishment until domes-
tic events took over and its origins were recalled.
As similar places like Devil's Island and Alcatraz
in the Americas were becoming mere memories,
Robben reopened for business. Plucking nationalist troublemakers from their very home soil
seemed to be the ideal punishment and Robben
was the ideal spot. Though South Africa owned
other islands, namely the Prince Edwards far to the
south, there were, as the world would later discover, separate plans for them.

And so the first wave of modern Robben-
Islanders had materialised in the early 1960s with
Mandela and the so-called Rivonia defendants, to
be followed by others by the hundred. Men not
only from the ANC, though that was the biggest
through having the broadest appeal, but from the

Pan-African Congress and later the South West African People's Organisation from Namibia. There would be names like Sisulu, Mbeki, Mostaledi, Mhlaba and, in 1966, Ja Toivo the SWAPO leader and Mandela's equivalent.

Then, in 1969, less than a year after graduation in London, it was my turn.

Plenty of other Islanders, the aforementioned Mbeki and Sisulu, along with Maharaj, Dingake, Nkosi, Kantor and of course Mandela himself, have related their experiences and to be sort of poetic, they have more right to write about the place than me. Most of those guys had been there for over five years and were almost an aristocracy. All highly educated men, many with degrees and doctorates, they outclassed their warders at everything except worldly status.

I had been picked up in Transkei, shortly after being reunited with my family and there had been time to pay my respects at Chief Luthuli's grave. There had been new additions to my police dossier while I had been overseas. Leaving the country was a serious offence in itself and that, coupled with education at the infamous LSE, made me a more dangerous animal than ever. When I picked up the threads of political activity enemies were close at hand. I was perfect material for the Suppression of Communism Act. The sentence of one thousand days sounded almost regal. It meant I would be entering the next decade inside a cell.

Again my wife and children watched me being led away by snarling men and dogs, this time to an airstrip. I was emplaned to the Cape and embarked at the harbour, Cape Town itself like a twinkling paradise all round. The boat was old and rusting, in contrast to the gleaming SAN patrol boat which was the escort. I was placed below decks for the crossing.

In that guy Dumas' *Count of Monte Cristo* the hero at least got a chance to stare up at the approaching outline of his Chateau d'Ifre; for me there was no such luxury, no general canvas for my eye to take in. A group of combined ANC-SWAPO, we unloaded on the small dock. We got a glimpse of white rock and a gun emplacement and then were hustled into cells. At that time there were still black warders but the Boers called the shots. We were put into the 'Zinc block', the temporary wing, but the pattern of permanent life was soon unravelled clear as a bell. A bell it was, noisy and deliberately jangling, that woke us every day at 5.30 a.m. Then would come the grim mealie breakfast and the aimless waiting, broken only by the labour shifts in the open air that took just two forms; quarrying or guano-gathering. The first meant the mile walk to the white quarry and then the work with the hammer. Hard labour, but it toned up the muscles, kept you fit and focused your immediate thoughts, though it gradually all but broke your back. And then the soft labour, the gathering of seabird-excreta, made you pull an agonised face with the stink and insiduously added to the ache in your spine.

You could also jog if you had the strength left, and read and study, but at all times you saw the hand of cynical authoritarianism. They tried to divide and rule. Separate prisoners' clothing was one stunt; Indians, coloureds and blacks, with guess-who at the bottom of the heap. And there was the reading material; despite their lauded Puritanism, the guards made sure there was plenty of non-serious literature, especially sexual, to try and undermine moral fibre. The older prisoner-aristocrats knew all these tricks but newcomers found it all very destructive. Some fresh arrivals, though, reckoned they had new tricks up their sleeve. Even on Robben Island, as in every prison from time immemorial, that six-letter word had been uttered—E-S-C-A-P-E.

Only one man had been known ever to have got away from Robben and that had been Herri, the very first inmate back in the seventeenth century. He had apparently simply stolen a Dutch boat and paddled to shore to disappear into the interior, but there had never been a repeat. Certain fellow-convicts wondered all the same. Others told them they were reaching for the moon. And yet in 1969 that moon *had* been reached, albeit by white guys in white spacesuits.

Some guys laid elaborate plans. There was the SWAPO guy—I'll call him Joachim—who came from north-east Namibia in the region called

109

Kaokoland. He spoke both English and German besides his native tongue. He did not, rightly, consider himself a South African and believed that if he could make it home he would be safe, despite the occupation by Boer troops. His idea was simply to copy Herri and steal a boat. It would have to be in July, when the Benguela current swept past Robben for the north and the Fish River estuary. Once on Namibian soil, Joachim reckoned he was home and dry.

A gang of us discussed it and I put in that a better idea, if a boat could be had, would be to head for the shipping lanes to the west and hope to be picked up by a friendly crew. Another guy suggested simply swimming for the mainland. Someone else estimated that given the Benguela and the sharks, he would have managed about a hundred strokes and no more. Another in the gang, a diehard Communist, had an implicit faith in Russians coming to help. His notion was that Soviet seaplanes hung around the Island in case of escaping prisoners. It was in fact true that the Russian navy were by 1970 almost the only navy in the world to have retained large flying-boats, but I thought the likelihood of white or rather red knights in the vicinity highly unlikely.

But the grab-a-boat idea still hung around as the months passed. We knew there must be constant crossings over False Bay to the mainland bringing fresh supplies and shifts of warders, but we didn't know the layout of the docks. We hardly

110

got to glimpse much sea, and that was usually
sandwiched between guards and their watchtower.
Later Joachim added to his idea. It had come to
him while we were working in the quarry in blazing heat, half-blinded by the glare. We would pass
ourselves off as guards, literally whiten ourselves
up with the lime, use shovels as guns-from-a-
distance and charge for the harbour, then we could
commandeer a vessel. I thought it was imaginative, but it withered in the reality of guards and
their Brownings, not to mention patrol boats.
Which gave Joachim the idea of storming a patrol
boat. Which made me cite the warships of the
SAN fleet just along the coast at Simonstown.
Joachim swore at me all that day.

To be fair, there could have been the chance of a
quarry-break in very freak weather, say a sudden
fogbank or a downpour, but I had doubts about the
sea ever being reached. In such weather it would
usually be the time of year when the Benguela was
flowing south for the Antarctic. But even the South
Pole became a possibility to Joachim. That, or one
of the foreign islands, British Tristan da Cunha or
the Norwegian-owned territory nearby. Some of
us kept a close eye on Joachim, knowing that a
moment of madness could lead to a bloodbath in
the quarry. A big Ciskeian, who had once been a
policeman before ANC involvement, made sure he
was close by the Namibian whenever the weather
closed in or the guards looked lax, which was a
very rare occurrence.

Me, I knew too much about the ways of the sea with my Wild Coast background. Me, my escape route was into the mind—reading and writing. Our access to material had improved by '71 and I devoured more classics, as well as sharpening my economics training. I came up with a major thesis on the cost of actually running Robben, from warders' salaries—they were now all white—to maritime fuel costs, to food. Against that I listed the mining profits of limestone and guano. Hmm. I thought about drafting a letter to Pretoria. You could of course read economics into everything, even the crudely censored magazines. Others of my batch slowly followed suit, though I don't think it was because of my example. We had nothing else, no visits, although Winnie Mandela had been allowed onto Robben around that time. In that guy Dumas' Monte Cristo story, the hero's fellow-prisoner pointed at his four walls and described *them* as his university. That was what Mandela was doing, using his brain instead of banging it against a brick wall—before, during and after my stay.

It was much later that I learnt of the viable escape plan that had existed, concerning Mandela. British sympathisers had apparently schemed to use a round-the-world air race as cover, with the famous aviatrix Sheila Scott landing near the island and whisking Mandela off to freedom.

I never quite believed it. It sounded like a Joachim concoction. In any case, Mandela would not have gone, neither in the sixties nor the seventies. His task was to sit tight. Robben I guess was a university all right, a seat of learning, though I often wondered what the guards learnt. There was another French prison book I read a long time later concerning Devil's Island, in which a guy said it was bad enough being a prisoner but at least it was one better than being a warder. I knew what he meant. Better to be wronged than doing the wronging. At that time plenty of guards were sleeping untroubled, though. They thought they were doing their job and making us tame. When my batch was released in late 1971 after completing our thousand-day term, we probably looked tamed. We were landed on the mainland in a squall, some of us suffering *mal de mer*. I saw several guards grin to one another.

'Sick as pigs, those kaffirs,' I heard one say. 'They won't stray far from now on.'

As a matter of fact, I was just about to start the ANC missions that would have me crossing much more water, from rivers to lakes to complete oceans.

8

Zambia

<u>   </u>

*T*he most important Frontline states facing White
Africa were sometimes called the 'Big Five' after
the leading wild animals such as the lion and the
rhino. For us, the king of the beasts was Zambia.

Independent in 1964 after a successful campaign of civil disobedience, it had been one of 'the
Rhodesias' complete with a sizeable white population. Some of those whites had been less than gra-
cious; on the very first morning of self-government
the specially commissioned giant statue of an
African ripping off wristchains was unveiled, only
to show that some wise guy had daubed the message 'BLACKS'LL BREAK ANYTHING.' More
charitably, nearby graffiti had stated 'IF YOU FIND
YOURSELF IN TROUBLE THERE'S ALWAYS THE
COPPER', which was a reference not to police
assistance but to Zambia's most valuable mineral
asset. Outrightly hostile Europeans had left in
droves for neighbouring countries, especially the
other portion of the Rhodesias that intended to
retain the name in the singular.

Given this, there was a raising of hackles between President Kenneth Kaunda and his white counterpart from the start. Like feuding brothers, each made his moves. When Rhodesian black nationalist parties like ZANU were banned, Kaunda offered them haven and extended the hospitality to the South African ANC. Ian Smith then accepted military aid from Pretoria. Kaunda then allowed further guerrilla bases. The common border had already been closed, which had hit Zambia's copper market the hardest. But the lines were drawn. There were within a few years nearly a hundred guerrilla camps the length and breadth of Zambia's countryside, which was of similar size to neighbouring Portuguese Mozambique to the east. Three vast radio stations had been erected with Kaunda's permission to pump out propaganda at the white states all around them, but it had only isolated the Zambians even more.

And then in the mid-seventies had come the turnaround. Mozambique, and Angola on Zambia's western border, had been relinquished by the Portuguese and the 'Bamboo Line' had been completed, to provide the means of export for the copper. Suddenly Rhodesia was the surrounded country. South African military assistance had been officially withdrawn. Then the Rhodesians had caught their breath and laughed. In Zambia itself, despite all the advances, dissension appeared within the hundred guerrilla camps. The two main groups, Joshua Nkomo's ZAPU and Robert

Mugabe's ZANU, had begun feuding along old tribal lines; the former was Matabele and the other Shona, from the east of Rhodesia. The Zambian army was forced to intervene. The Rhodesians, who had always ridiculed Zambians, found the situation quite typical. On the common border across the Zambezi, white soldiers would shout insults, knowing the Zambians spoke English. One favourite jibe was calling Kaunda's soldiers, given their political leanings, the Marx Brothers.

The squabbling within the guerrilla groups continued, until Mugabe's ZANU moved out to set up bases in newly-friendly Mozambique. ANC guys like me had watched all this, but we made it our business to get on with both factions. We needed all the help we could get, whatever and wherever, but our main grouping remained in Zambia in co-operation with ZIPRA, the ZAPU military wing.

I was in Zambia on around twenty occasions, at first doing basic military training and then dealing with logistics. The Bamboo Line ran down through Zambia and touched a corner of Botswana, where a ferry, known as the 'Freedom Ferry' operated and brought things closer to the South African border. Zambia was thus at the heart of the supply line and for a logistics officer it was the place to be. The Rhodesians knew all about it, but they were at first more concerned with their eastern border and Mugabe's ZANLA and for quite a few months we were left in peace. My main work area was the big guerrilla base at Chikumbi, just north of the Zambian capital Lusaka. I noticed ZIPRA was receiving more arms and becoming very regular-style, to the point of smart uniforms and heavy weapons. It was the use of such weaponry, SAM 7s, surface-to-air missiles, that finally attracted Rhodesian attention to Zambia.

Chikumbi camp was hit on 19 October 1978. The airspace had been secured by Rhodesia who had warned the Zambian air force at all these bases to stay grounded if they knew what was good for them. The Zambians obeyed for three full days, by which time a thousand guerrillas had been killed. The targeted men were not only ZIPRA, but ANC and SWAPO. Two other nearby camps, Mborama and Mkushi, were also taken out. I was at a camp in the southwest, near the Zambezi, so I missed it. We quickly knew the main culprits had been the Rhodesian infantry, but they would have been spearheaded by a unit which was very much on a par with the Israelis of Entebbe.

The Rhodesian SAS had been born out of the British regiment, having served with it in fifties Malaya. It learnt the counterinsurgency business the hard way, making deep jungle penetrations and targeting leaders in their lairs. The Rhodesians had continued links with Britain into the sixties, joining it on tours in Aden. Their tactics were to make lightning assaults with explosives and retire leaving very clever booby traps. All were white, and some were British or Australian, besides Rhodesian. They would smear themselves with black cream to look more African than an African. So any white face found in a target area could only be a Communist adviser and was thus fair game to them.

As I say, I missed the Chikumbi raid, and the one later on Lusaka itself, when the SAS actually went into Nkomo's residence on an assassination mission. My big night was near the shores of Lake Kariba.

A man-made sheet of water between Rhodesia and Zambia created by the Kariba Dam, the lake's centre was the international border. By water was the way the raiders came that night. I was woken up in my tent by distant blasts. I got dressed, grabbed my AK-47 and a dozen ANC and led them on foot to an adjacent camp manned by a unit of the Zambia regiment. Fortunately I had my ID tag on. We were nearly shot. A Zambian officer appeared and we spoke in English. We could see distant flames along the lake.

'Livingstone. They're hitting Livingstone, lieutenant,' he said. He had a Sandhurst accent and did not use the comrade-prefix. He was leading a reaction unit to try and cut off the raiders' retreat. He wanted volunteers. I vounteered my men and we clambered aboard a large army truck and headed along the lakeside. I stayed on the running board. We could see flares and tracers, a lot of it reflected in the lake. It looked to me like panic-firing. We rounded a bend and found another Zambian personnel carrier on its side. Two soldiers lay badly injured. We left them to a medical team and went inland through trees. There was a smell of cordite and burning. We used torches sparingly. We came upon smouldering bushes, spent bullet cases and a dead monkey who had obviously appeared at the wrong time.

We heard distant engines as we came out onto the lake. I saw a fleck of foam. The raiders had obviously used fast assault-craft and I was watching them head for their side of Kariba. Some more Zambian soldiers appeared and I yelled in time to stop a tragic firefight. We all stared south and the officer-in-charge pointed excitedly at a spotlight. A Zambian vessel, one of the lake's old pleasurecraft-turned-gunboat, was giving chase. It had powerful engines and it had a good chance. I wondered if any of the raiders had been behind schedule and was swimming for his life.

We waited on the shore and watched the spotlight dart across the water and saw flares being fired. There was a burst of distant tracer from the gunboat, another flare and then silence. It returned at daybreak with its catch.

The spotlight had apparently picked out an object of terror. A black globe was floating towards them, obviously despatched by the raiders. The gunboat officer had ordered a burst and then screamed a stop as the globe had closed with his bows. The officer and an NCO had bravely gone forward with poles.

Then the spotlight had picked up the ugly object, clear as a bell. The officer had ordered 'stop engines' and waited for light. He had reached over the side. He picked up a large rubber beach-ball with the bootblack on it already wearing off. Chalked in English were letters saying, 'IT'S NOT A MINE. IT'S A-YOURS.'

Their humour wasn't bad, their troops weren't bad, but it still didn't mean that good was necessarily on their side.

9

The American Skyline

*A*lmost as a reward for the Robben Island years, I was to my surprise given the opportunity of advancing the ANC cause by petitioning at the United Nations, which would mean a journey to the United States.

After all those times swinging the hammer in that quarry, I had taken away some of the rock in my heart. I was hardened-ANC now. Not long after returning to Transkei I had been imprisoned yet again, this time for 180 days or six months at Victor Verster prison outside Pretoria. This time it had hardly affected me. At least I knew my cell was also a potential office or study-room. There was no need to look over my shoulder—it had already happened—and I knew where my next meal was coming from, namely the prison kitchens. I even recruited certain warders to the cause.

As it happened, the end of my sentence at Verster coincided with an ideal time for a political offensive at the UN. The Arabs, after having lost the Yom Kippur war in 1973 when they had begun so triumphantly, had taken out their anger on the Western world by trebling oil prices. Countries from Britain to France to South Africa to the United States were having to take the effects on the chin. The oil-producing countries, including African states, were flexing political muscle and for liberation movements like the ANC there was suddenly no better time to make inroads and ask favours. Even America itself, with the inconclusiveness in Vietnam, was not quite the same Colossus.

A quick briefing with an ANC man in Johannesburg, and the air-trip was all arranged. A former preacher, B.Sc. and Robben-Islander was deemed an ideal representative. I did the Botswana thing again in a near-repeat of my trip the six years before, except this time I stayed on the plane at Heathrow. This time my tickets bore the initials JFK, the international airport serving New York. I smiled most of the way across the Atlantic, comparing the lavish meals with the prison slop and the seats with cell-mats. And I had to admit it, but the omnipresent figures in uniform were just that bit more appealing. Names like Jenny and Sue had the edge over Jan and Jakob. And then my pretty hostesses were telling me to look out my porthole. Staten, Manhattan . . . every island I could see was a jewel compared with that ugly spot on the Cape.

The jumbo circled me over and into Kennedy where people were waiting. One of them was the ANC's permanent representative at the UN.

Another was a US Customs official, a smiling long-haired man. Long hair amazed me. It was everywhere. I had seen its wild beginnings in sixties London and now it was accepted in the conservative states, while back in South Africa it had been military haircuts or shaven heads all around.

I was reminded of London and Ram's warning when I noticed two crewcuts in suits beside Customs, watching me. Maybe American security people sat up when guys like me jetted in. The ANC representative didn't seem worried and put me at my ease. He was my host and he knew his Big Apple. Our cab took us through Queens and Brooklyn Bridge and there it was, the whole famous skyline glittering in the winter afternoon. There were the new twin towers of the World Trade Centre and the Empire State, and below that the UN itself. We crossed the bridge to First Avenue. My host was well-educated, American-educated and in an American-style suit to look the part. I was in an old coat but I was not ungrateful in the biting cold that even the taxi's heater couldn't beat. The coat got further creases as I looked out the rear.

'There's nobody following, Joe,' my host said affably. 'It's safe and clean here.'

Clean it was in the smart Fifth Avenue tailor's where I was bought a new suit to look the political part . . . but safe? That evening we went for a look 'uptown' at black Harlem. We looked like any other residents, I suppose, albeit well-dressed.

And we stayed in the cab. I didn't like what I saw. South African cities were clean, if on the backs of an African workforce, but sparkling and safe-looking. 1967 London had been quaint with only a few highrises, but this . . . ? I felt uncomfortable with New York.

'They were definitely here first, unlike back home,' I commented to my host. 'Peter Stuyvesant, New Amsterdam, even the name Harlem. Maybe we can blame *them* for this.'

My fellow South African looked perplexed. 'Blame who, Joe?'

'The Dutch of course,' I said.

The UN General Assembly building which we visited two days later as part of the official ANC delegation was not unimpressive, but it wasn't me. However, I hadn't come thousands of airmiles to sightsee or pass an opinion. My business was to help the delegates lobby the right sort of people. OK, it was impressive, the multicoloured people, the planet Earth in microcosm, but it was really just another office for business.

We got down to business. I carried the economics portfolio and supplied information that had been prepared for me, adding a few suggestions myself. It was all very formal and I noticed similar groups here on the same mission. There were guys from SWAPO here about Resolution 385, the relinquishment of Namibia which South Africa was illegally resisting. There were the Rhodesian Patriotic Front groups, at that time quite united.

There were anti-Portuguese-Africa groups and there was even POLISARIO from the Spanish Sahara. The big buzz was that we might knock South Africa off its seat on the General Assembly. Another buzz was that the PLO's Yasser Arafat might be visiting to address this same Assembly. It was all very impressively seductive, but it sobered me to think that with all this palatialness our own leader, my own clansman, was sitting at this same moment on a former leper colony as though he too had the disease.

Our permanent representative knew that too. His good suit and Americanisms were all part of the job but no more. I quickly discerned other things besides well-meaning idealism. I could see pride, nepotism, corruptiveness, elitism and not a little of it was visible on the African benches. I was relieved to think we were nowhere near that stage. We were the lowest of the low, at ground level, but playing the diplomatic game at the starting point. We were here to prick the world's conscience as deeply as we could.

Some people though, here in the land of the Ku Klux Klan, were unprickable. The PR nodded to some hardfaced guys with fair hair and dark suits. There were opposing camps in position, too—emissaries from Pretoria here to court American rightwing pressure groups. I got a hard look from a blond guy in a bar. It kept me on my toes and gave me strength when the time came to speak to people. The portfolio aside, I was questioned by dozens of people about life on Robben Island and this man Nelson Mandela. And I answered the same questions on my second visit to the UN. And the third.

And then the PR told me I had done enough. The fresh ripples had been made and now the professionals could take over. The long debates would resume. I had caused enough interest and could think about going home. I was thanked for all the help and there was to be another reward.

My air ticket, my Delta, allowed me further travel in the United States and I could take a look elsewhere. The PR had noticed I hadn't been that taken with New York itself and suggested I could fly to a more congenial neck of the woods. The sky was the limit for the next seven days. I could go perhaps to Washington if I wished, the capital itself that held a predominantly black population. Or I could visit Chicago, or Detroit-Motown. Or I could try the Deep South—Alabama where so much civil rights history had been made, or Little Rock. Or the cradle of so much Afro-American culture, New Orleans. Or a meeting with the Black Panthers could be arranged.

I shook my head with a smile. I knew exactly what part of America I wanted to see and it had the most natural of skylines. It was moreover pure white in colour. It was the Rocky Mountain range. I hadn't forgotten my boyhood view of the snowy Drakensberg.

I flew to Denver, Colorado, into a world of

snow. It was a winter wonderland, and wondrous
things happened. I hired a car easily, even though
I didn't have proper international papers. I got
myself a jeep and took off for the skyline. This
was the America I fell for, although there are very
few black guys resident in Colorado. Locals were
friendly despite that, or because of it. Did I want
to visit the Grand Canyon in the south? No, I
didn't, because we had a near-replica much closer
to home in Namibia. How about Beecher Island to
the east? I was asked. This was the stuff of that
guy Burt Lancaster: US army scouts attacked by a
thousand Indians in 1868 and making a last stand
on a river island had been rescued by the Tenth
Cavalry, a famous all-black regiment. I said no
thank you and drove off for another day in the
mountains. Someone else told me these peaks and
the plains before them had been the 'Great
American Desert', an uncrossable barrier which
had kept white settlers back for years before the
truth came out, just as legends of the Sahara had
delayed the proper European conquest of southern
Africa and kept the Boers in their time-warp.

I came upon a real barrier when driving south
to a town called Colorado Springs. I took a mountain trail and suddenly there was a fence and soldiers. More soldiers appeared and waved me off,
but not before I had seen a whole military convoy
appear on another mountain road. I saw a
squadron of helicopters overfly the mountains and
land nearby, all of which gave me an eerie feeling.

Returning to the main road I drove into Colorado Springs and stopped at a garage where a young girl was in charge of the petrol pumps. She turned down her transistor radio at my question and smiled up to a very distant peak.

'Don't you know about Cheyenne Mountain up there, mister?' she said.

I soon found out. Of all the towns in that state and of all the states in that entire country, I had approached the most militarily-sensitive, the actual command post for the defence of North America in time of all-out war, a post buried Rip-van-Winkle-like deep within a missile-proof mountain cave.

A few days later I flew back to the east coast and then the Atlantic, unaware that in a few years' time I would be near another command post where around us the closest thing to an all-out African war was being waged—complete with tanks, missiles and even airborne assault. I would go into Angola five times.

10

Angola

---

*T*he Angolan front had come like a bolt from the blue to everyone in southern Africa. Blacks and whites, soldiers and guerrillas alike, had been dumbstruck. In 1974, Portuguese Africa had suddenly decided to disband itself. Along with Mozambique, Guinea and a few islands, Angola was to be handed over to nationalists who had been fighting for independence since the sixties. Angola had seen the first colonial presence in Africa, established even before Columbus, and had carried on through the centuries in a sort of sleepwalk, avoiding world wars and winds of change and even containing the first rebelliousness inspired by the nearby Congo. But the containment had proved costlier with the years and more unpopular with the conscripts from Europe. Until, with the other colonies similarly engaged, disenchantment and then revolution had come to Portugal itself. The chief instigator had been the most unlikely revolutionary. General Manuel di Spinola, a commander-in-chief with Prussian looks complete with monocle, had cried 'enough'. And so the liners and troopships had sailed back to Lisbon taking five hundred years of history with them, and effectively reducing the size of White Africa by sixty per cent.

Angola itself, with an even larger land area than South Africa, was independent within the year, but its real fighting had only just begun. Such had been the speed of the Portuguese exodus that no clear government had taken over. The guerrilla groups, with the main prey gone, had turned on themselves. The MPLA, the FNLA and UNITA were the main opponents, the former Marxists and the others more conservative. Civil war had broken out even before proper independence and the MPLA had won, despite the others receiving South African help. It had been the familiar left-versus-right fight.

Caught in the middle had been SWAPO, the Namibian guerrilla movement that had been waging an insurgency campaign in its homeland from Angolan bases, and along with them some ANC. With the civil war, UNITA moved closer to South Africa's side, which had pushed us in the direction of the Angolan government of President Agostinho Neto. And the war had not ended. UNITA had taken to the vast bush in the south and with continuing Boer backup was harrying not only Angolans but SWAPO-ANC. It was the 'My enemy is that man's enemy so we are allies' story again. But the real heavyweight friend of the

Luanda government, the one that had tipped the scales in the original fighting, had not been African at all.

Fidel Castro's Cuba had been the new player. The island that had been the cause of John Kennedy's nuclear gamble had sent thousands of its men to Africa in a massive military buildup. From coastal railheads like Mocamedes and Benguela, supplies and equipment had poured in to underpin the Cuban presence. By 1977, when Castro himself visited Angola, Spanish speakers were part of the landscape.

It was soon after Castro's tour that I came to Angola, though there was no fanfare. The job was supervising supply-routes for SWAPO-ANC camps near the border. At the time I visited, well to the rear of the Angolan-Namibian border, not much notice was taken of the occasional South African Mirage that flew high overhead. My actual base was at Cassinga, which was the main SWAPO command post in southern Angola. Cassinga was sited near the main coastal railway and, nearly five hundred miles from the nearest South African soldier, was deemed quite safe. There was also a mass of forward camps in between, with thousands of SWAPO, ANC, Angolan and Cuban troops. Our side was the one making the running, and had been building up for most of the previous year, infiltrating men into the Namibian regions of Ovambo and the Caprivi Strip and giving the Boers headaches by the score. South African troops had not set foot inside Angola in the two years since the end of the civil war and if they did, the border camps would act as tripwires and give plenty of warning.

It was at Cassinga that I got to know my first real Cuban. His name was Captain Esteban. He was, like so many of his brother-officers, a near-replica of Castro himself. He had the same olive battledress and stiff cap, the same Andalusian features although cleanshaven and the same teeth-clenched Havanas. Captain Esteban was around my age but had spent his years rising through the ranks of his army. I spoke no Spanish so our conversation was in English, and his came with an American accent—which was ironic, for he harboured a pathological hate for his island's huge northern neighbour. Esteban had helped face that neighbour's proxy invasion at the Bay of Pigs when just a mere militiaman and he believed that by coming here to Angola he was fighting that same war. The South African and the *Yanqui* were just the same. During that conversation I decided not to mention my regard for John Kennedy, although I was now of course no friend of Uncle Sam myself.

Esteban reminded me during a meal at the officers' mess in Cassinga—I was of course in camouflage uniform—that Cubans were here as liberators and had a clean conscience concerning Africa with no history of colonialism, although an expert might have argued that Cuba when part of the Spanish

Empire had benefited from slave labour on their sugar plantations. I had noticed as a further reminder of those days that some of Esteban's men were more black than white. Usually, though, I made it my business to get on with officers, knowing goodwill brought extra dividends. I answered some of Esteban's questions about my background. My having been to Europe and America fascinated him, though he looked totally uninterested when I talked of my time as a minister.

He became friendly enough to invite me on a visit to some of the forward SWAPO camps at Chetaquera, which was within twenty miles of the Namibian border. And there, he gave me a grin, lit his third cigar of the day and suggested we could go for an even closer look if I fancied. There was no risk and it might be a bit of excitement.

We went next day, by truck and then on foot. We had two guides, one SWAPO and the other Angolan. They took us along an old animal trail and then a dried-up river. The country here was as dry as a bone, a world away from the Transkei's lush hilliness. The trees were stunted, with only palms standing truly upright.

Then we halted by the river. Using fieldglasses I focused over a barrier and saw my first South African soldiers in a long time. They were tankmen, manning an *Olifant* or Elephant, which was parked under a palm-tree for shade. Under nearby trees I could see their support infantry. They were in nut-brown uniforms with soft hats and were hardly moving in the midday heat. As always this was the best time for black guys to be active.

It should have come as no surprise when a line of black soldiers appeared on foot, oblivious to the sun, except they too were in SA uniform.

'*Policia. Policia negra.*' Esteban pulled on yet another Havana in disgust as he lay alongside. The black guys were apparently special constables from the local Ovambo tribe, a tribe SWAPO was trying to subvert. They sat crosslegged in the open and in a moment more vehicles appeared behind. One was a Hippo but the carrier behind was new to me.

It was new to Esteban too. It looked like a rocket-launcher, the Russian-made weapons used by our side. Esteban made a diagram on his map-case as we watched. Smoke wafted. They were brewing up tea. We watched the enemy for an hour and wildlife also came into view. A herd of gemsbok came along the river and then darted off, scenting us, or more likely Esteban's cigar. Then came doglike shapes, jackals or hyenas. When real dogs could be heard barking, I wondered if we should move. We all knew the sound of Alsatian trackers and they were in the vicinity. I noticed several of the Ovambo police stare over, perhaps aware of our presence.

Esteban relit his cigar as he finished his sketch of the rocket-launcher.

'*No pasaran, camarada.*' He used a famous

Marxist slogan. 'They will not pass. They won't dare come over. We, you and I, make the running now.'

There was a howl behind. One of the nearby jackals was answering the tracker-dogs beyond the barrier and it sounded eerie. Esteban threw down his cigar and nodded to the SWAPO scout to extricate us.

So the front looked quiet. We returned to the rear where by contrast there was a hive of activity, with more weapons and ammunition reaching the forward camps, where in their turn infiltration groups would be primed to slip over that fence we had seen. I busied myself helping and learning higher logistics as the end of April approached.

It was at the beginning of the new month, May Day 1978, that I got a surprise from Captain Esteban. A number of advisors, Russians and Cubans, had got in a celebratory mood with drink. Some Africans had joined them but I stayed aloof. For one, there was more overseeing to do at the railhead and for another they were drinking vodka and I was a brandy man. I was seated happily in a camouflage tent when Esteban appeared, with the inevitable cigar, and a colourless bottle in one hand. He was quite drunk, and seemed curiously lonely.

'Celebrate May Day, *camarada*. Come on.'

I shook my head politely and looked up at a distant vapour trail. It was not one of our Migs. The trail was southerly, meaning a Mirage.

'Celebrate something else then, *camarada*. Your birthday near?'

I smiled and told him the date.

'Born New Year's Day.' He looked wistful and downed more vodka. 'Me, I was born on the day of my namesake. True, Comrade Miwe.'

I didn't understand a moment and he took his cap off and bowed his head.

'The Feast of Stephen. The day of Stephen, Saint Stephen. You understand, *camarada*?'

I understood. St Stephen's was the day after Christmas, Boxing Day. Esteban knew his saints. He had obviously once been a Roman Catholic like all Cubans before Castro. There were army dog-tags round his neck now where a crucifix had probably once hung. I grinned. He was an atheist and a believer in the ascendancy of Marxist-Leninism. Like me. I put down my papers.

'Okay, I'll try this vodka, comrade captain.'

I took a long swig of his bottle though I closed my eyes at the taste. Esteban gave a giggle and forced more of the bottle on me and I saw up into the sky through the glass. The Mirage was circling high above.

The next day I suffered a hangover, but Esteban was obviously used to vodka and was a hive of activity, taking over some of my duties. I reciprocated the next day. Lorried supplies from the railhead at Serpa Pinto sometimes beat the train deliveries. With my love of driving, I volunteered. The transport was a Ural truck. I left for Serpa

Pinto, crossing the Cubango river. I stayed the night, and left at first light to return to Cassinga and Captain Esteban. We had spoken by radio and we had another party in store in a few days to celebrate another famous victory for the Marxist world, the twenty-fourth anniversary of the fall of Dienbienphu. Among the SWAPO supplies were more vodka and cigars for the Cuban advisers.

We were about five miles from Cassinga when I saw the black smoke on the horizon ahead. At first I thought there had been a fire, some accident at the command post. Then an Angolan soldier pointed to the glints. I realised Mirages had come back and were here in force. Cassinga was under air attack. We speeded up, watching the black pyres grow and then using glasses I spotted several white puffs. Parachutes. Some of the convoy gave a cheer, believing some Mirages had been downed and their pilots had ejected. And then we saw more and more patches of white in the Angolan sky. I felt the hairs on the back of my neck. Cassinga was under airborne assault. Those Mirage spotters had seen the buildup of supplies for an obvious SWAPO infiltration campaign and it was being nailed right on the head.

An Angolan officer halted the convoy, which was exactly my thinking. It would be like trundling in fresh targets. We waited in the bush, watching the southern horizon turn totally black. The ground shook under distant blasts as arms dumps went up. We waited with weapons cocked.

Things broke from cover. Wild animals. Birds flew. An ostrich charged past, then some bucks. The ground shuddered again. We swung and saw a group of tanks, T54s crewed by Angolans with a Cuban major. They were going to counterattack. The paratroopers mopping up Cassinga would be lightly-armed. I volunteered to join the infantry to ride on the tanks but instead of warmly welcoming us the Cuban officer, already shocked by what was happening, became paranoiac. He demanded to check my identity in case we were UNITA. Finally satisfied, he allowed a dozen of us aboard, leaving the convoy ironically in laager formation as Boers would have done.

The T54s trundled forward at about twenty miles an hour and we were treated to more pyrotechnics ahead. It was obvious Cassinga was being gutted, but maybe we could get revenge on the paratroopers. The Cuban ordered more speed and we fanned out, going through bushes and bull-dozing huge maklani palms. As one such tree col-lapsed ahead of us its shaking fronds were replaced by new whirling on the skyline. Helicopters. That was how the paratroopers were being pulled out. More of them appeared, less than three miles away, their pilots entering the smoke palls. They were bigger than Alouettes, probably Pumas. The major ordered more speed, aiming his pistol through his hatch at the Angolan driver and swearing in Spanish. The T54 revved and tore away bushes revealing a herd of bucks which scattered. Several were hit by the tank, squealing. I heard another din. Mirages again. Coming in to cover the Pumas. I saw a streak in the sky and air-to-ground missiles slammed in. More palms toppled, birds flew everywhere and I felt the ground shake.

The Cuban major was enraged. His driver had stalled. He cursed again and dropped down, pulling the hatch behind and next second the vehicle was off again, with maybe the officer himself at the controls. Despite his rage he was too slow. I could see the Pumas lifting off now, each obviously with its group of smoke-blackened raiders. Another Mirage appeared and fired a burst of cannon, setting a nearby copse ablaze and then it was gone and we were re-entering Cassinga.

It had been razed. Six months of logistics work had gone literally up in smoke. Thousands, millions of rounds of ammunition were still exploding as he sifted through. There were bodies everywhere, most of them African, most of them further blackened by flames. Charred papers were scattered in all directions, some still in the air. The downdraughts from the Pumas had fanned the fires. I saw bits of priceless documents, maps, information in tiny bits. More T54s trundled in. A whole Angolan tank brigade had arrived, but too late. I saw a familar box on the ground and whisked it away just before heavy tracks crushed it, though it could have been a booby trap. It was a harmless wooden box of cigars. They said '*Romeo y*

Julieta'. Those were the sort that Captain Esteban had smoked. I looked around as bodies were lined up. There were some whites among the dead, but thankfully no sign of Esteban. Maybe he had been nearer the border. My heart sank as we heard further news. The border camps at Chetaquera had been simultaneously hit, this time by direct ground forces. *Olifant* tanks had overrun the lightly armed bases and put more supplies to the torch, blasting out hundreds of men.

I never discovered what had happened to Esteban, whether he had been at a forward camp or at Cassinga, or whether he would see another St Stephen's day. Cuban sources clamped a veil over information concerning individuals and I was informed I should be more objective and less subjective in my thinking.

Objectively speaking, 4 May 1978 had been a disaster for SWAPO. That one day had done months if not years of damage to the organisation. It had burnt away nearly all the infiltration lines into Namibia. Some of the SWAPO groups on the far side of the border were cut off without resupply and there would be no quick way to re-establish contact. Other logistical routes from the east, through the Caprivi Strip and Botswana, had been similarly dealt with in a concerted effort to stop SWAPO stone dead.

The raid had been codenamed 'Reindeer' after the most un-African of animals, but a Reindeer was also a beast of transport. It would be some time later during an emergency briefing that things would become *much* more subjective. An infiltration route would need to be blazed from a brand-new direction, the unlikeliest route of all. To blaze that trail, which would lead right into the very heart of the enemy's headquarters, SWAPO would ask the ANC for helpers and the ANC would select—well—me.

11

The School on the Black Sea

*L*ong before I had been to any fighting front, in fact shortly after basic training in 1976, I had again been sent out of Africa. This time my destination was not the Western world but the East. This was when I was first properly trained as a logistics officer. Somebody in the MK High Command had decided that a trained economist used to international travel would be ideal. For this I would have to undergo specalised instruction within the borders of our main backer, the Soviet Union. The rain was warm in Lusaka when I boarded an Aeroflot jet with my UN passport and an English-Russian dictionary, my most important possessions. It had turned to snow long before I reached Moscow. Looking out of my porthole I felt my blood shiver and remembered the American snow the few years before. There were no mountains directly below, though we had crossed coastal Turkey and the vast steppes were outstretched. I got a glimpse of the Olympic stadium they were constructing for the 1980 Games as we came into

the international runway north of the capital. The
wind cut me straight away, despite the thick coat.
In the VIP lounge an ANC man was waiting with a
thoughtful present, a fur cap. With him was a
Russian civilian, in fact a KGB colonel in plainclothes. At a briefing in Lusaka by one of our
political officers I knew already that there had been
an *Afrikaburo* within the KGB since the twenties.
One of the founders had been a black, a West
Indian named George Padmore. In the thirties
while I was still a child Padmore had come to
South Africa in the then-original guise of a chauffeur to set up communist cells. Padmore had
attained a KGB colonelcy, though he had originally
studied in the United States at Fisk University.

I had come here to study at the University of
Moscow. It was the oldest in Russia, having been
built in 1755 by the Czarina Elizabeth, daughter of
Peter the Great, but the University itself was actu-
ally known as the Lomonosov, after the first great
Russian scientist from her father's time. This
Lomonosov looked weirdly American at first sight.
It was a tall skyscraper built in 1953, the year of
Stalin's death. It would be the only high ground I
would occupy, the only thing nearing a Russian
mountain.

As at the LSE nearly ten years before, I kept my
head down and went into straight study. In
Moscow it was much easier with no 'swinging' dis-
tractions. Outside was too cold. I bookwormed
into the night in my dormitory, the fur hat still on

my head. The books shook in my hands, but I learnt more. Subjects included the history of guerrilla logistics, from the Ho Chi Minh trail that had run across the spine of Indochina to the 'Agostinho Neto' route that had run from East Africa into Angola during the anti-Portuguese struggle. Parts of the 'Neto' were in fact still in use. By now well-versed in finding irony, I noted that both those trails had depended largely on tree cover, while literally here in Moscow itself all the city trees had been felled during the thirties because of the risk of chemical attack, with clouds known to linger on leaves.

History and theory over, I studied elsewhere in Moscow, at the Military Academy. There was specialist training in arms and bombmaking. Then came more theory. Exhaustive geographical study. How to blaze supply trails. The aim was to avoid putting all the eggs in one basket. I was urged to be imaginative concerning routes. One day during a lecture with other students I had an idea.

'What about turning things on their head, comrade colonel?' I asked the lecturer. 'What about considering *us* having to cut guerrilla logistical lines? That would be a new angle.'

The room went colder than the ice on the windows. 'You mean guerrilla activity within Soviet borders, comrade Miwe?' the staff officer asked me. 'It is politically impossible. True freedom fighters are by definition Marxist.'

I felt slightly foolish and a nearby student

smiled. He was an Afghan officer. Neither of us was to know that within a few years Russian forces using everything from Hind gunships to Spetsnaz would be desperately trying to cut the logistical trails of the *Mujahideen*.

Shortly after that debate, though it was entirely coincidental, I was moved elsewhere to study. I went south, to the Black Sea and Odessa. It was like stepping into summertime. Although the area was a paradise, it had suffered like Moscow and Leningrad. Odessa was another 'Hero-city' which had endured an epic Nazi siege before falling. It was also where the battleship *Potemkin* had fired what were really the first shots of the Bolshevik Revolution. Standing on the famous Potemkin steps with my fur hat at last discarded, I was reminded of another curious link with home. The battleship's mutiny had come as a result of the Russian naval disaster of 1905. The Czar's fleet had sailed halfway round the world, refuelling at Luderitz near the Cape and then following the Wild Coast before crossing the Indian Ocean to meet its doom under Admiral Togo's torpedo-boats. Some of my clan, perhaps my grandfather with my own father in his arms, had watched the smoke of those proudly-passing funnels.

And now a new Russia was helping the descendants of those watchers. Except that Odessa was not really Russia at all. Ukrainians, I quickly learnt, were a different race entirely. I only showed passing interest; I had my own form of nationalism to think about. I attended Odessa University, another old Czarist building, although my principal place of study was the Patrice Lumumba wing. Other African radicals were here, but despite the socialism I spent little time socialising. Time was precious. ANC guys were dying back home, in and out of Frontline states, and I wanted to be there giving maximum assistance. The bits of trivia I picked up, such as the story of local guerrilla hero Stefan Bandera who had in the name of Ukrainian nationalism taken on the Nazis during the war and the Red Army after it, I kept trivial.

Some things made me pause though, such as hearing of the people on the eastern shore of the Black Sea who were black by race too; they were apparently descendants of African slaves brought back by Georgian princes in past centuries and could be found in the city of Sukhumi. Blacks of American birth were frequently featured in the propaganda films the Odessa students were shown, zeroing on the city ghettoes and the shacks of the Deep South. I watched a long sequence on New York, which I knew from firsthand experience was less than fair, but I found myself sharing in the classroom anger. Then came the sequences of 'hope': the Watts riots, the disgracing of Nixon, the T54s smashing into the Saigon embassy. Our heightened rage made us thirsty for more tuition, though outside the window the Black Sea sparkled ever more invitingly.

Odessa being a major naval base, we saw

plenty of warship activity and I got used to seeing the graceful flying boats which I gathered were called the *Tchaika* or 'Seagull'. I thought of that Robben Islander who would have swooned at such a sight. I also saw the freighters, bound for the Bosphorus and the Mediterranean, some of them carrying supplies for African movements. I carried on with studies with the sun warming me further and my teachers must have been satisfied that my course was being mindbent according to plan.

On a rare off-duty day, with my course at the Patrice Lumumba almost complete, I was allowed with some fellow students to go for a swim in the Black Sea. As an extra nugget we had been told that the Soviet leader Leonid Brezhnev himself had swum for his life in the same waters when as a commissar his landing-craft had been hit. I waded in and remembered home. The Wild Coast, though, with its treacherous shores, had no major port and thus also no chance of ever landing arms by boat for our struggle. I swam a long distance. I thought I could see the Anatolian mountains, but they could have been clouds.

I must have drifted some way because I realised I was heading back for the wrong beach. There was a red flag flying on shore which I hadn't seen before. Then I saw a fountain of water and another. I shook my head and altered course, doing a fast crawl towards my own beach. I learnt that the fountains had been caused by shots and that I had been directly offshore from a firing range

used by the *Moshin Nagant*, the naval infantry of
the Black Sea fleet. As once before, I had wandered
quite innocently into a target area, though this had
been over a mile offshore and the bullets largely
spent strays.

Back at Patrice Lumumba there was a final
examination in which the course was certified
brainwashed sparkling clean and I was awarded a
captaincy. As a last lesson, it was arranged that we
use that local naval infantry range for pistol practice, but on the appointed day there came an
unseasonal thunderstorm and the shoot was called
off.

Then the time came when I left Odessa for
Moscow International and the flight back to
Lusaka, before a more careful journey back across
several borders aiming for home.

There came a moment when, not long returned,
I sorely wished I had been able to familiarise
myself with the pistol on that Black Sea range. It
was when I was getting ready to shoot my way out
of a tight corner on the outskirts of South-West-
Town, a black satellite township that locals—and
by now the world—knew as Soweto.

12

Soweto

If 1963 had been the year for me of the series of
blows, then 1976 was the year of the one giant pul-
veriser. 16 June was the day it happened, when
South African security forces lost their temper with
a crowd of schoolchildren and opened fire with
high-powered weapons. Those children had been
unarmed, the only things in their hands the
Afrikaans books they were protesting about having
to study. Hundreds upon hundreds, still nobody
knows how many exactly, had been killed or
maimed. The troops had simply got angry at all
the black faces before them and had ignored the
shrillness of their shouts. Those kids had been
dressed in neat school clothes, in shorts and long
socks and shiny shoes—the same sort of uniform I
had first worn at Hill Down at around the same
age. I got angry too, and not just me. I looked at
my own two kids Thandi and Sandile in our home
in Transkei, thankfully far from Soweto,
Johannesburg, and I decided my new step. After
all my years in the ANC, suffering in all those

prisons and canvassing at the UN, I had still not done enough. I would go the whole hog. I had done the political, now it was the military mission.

I was far from alone. Over those mid-June evenings hundreds, thousands of guys were having exactly the same thoughts—Xhosa, Indian, Coloured . . . even whites. By the July, the ANC's Military Wing had quadrupled its numbers.

After the day of the shootings, the South African police and Defence Force troops had formed a ring of steel around Soweto, positioning their armoured vehicles—their Hippos and Rhinos and Buffalos—at all points of the compass, with men in riot gear, readied as shock troops.

For all the apologies to the world, the ring was still there a year later when I drove into the township. So was some of the smoke, with wreckage still smouldering and being relit in new incidents. By then I had had my Russian training and I had Russian guns in my 'bakkie', my pickup truck. Two dozen AK-47s and two thousand rounds of ammunition were a few metres behind me under a pile of fresh vegetables. I was alone; the incident with Nomuula by the Botswana border was still recent but I was determined to get something in, to give the folk some fightback if the Boers again lost their rag. Even though I still believed they would make mincemeat of any opposition, that they could shell and strafe and turn off water and electricity at the flick of a switch, I knew we couldn't be sitting ducks for ever and even if a few scores were settled it was better than none at all.

So I was helping plant a small arsenal inside Soweto but it was still as risky as ever. Despite the infiltrations and the gun-runs to elsewhere in the RSA, Soweto was still the tinder-box, ready to go up again. The people inside were the most volatile, the most aggrieved, the most dangerous. Even Winnie Mandela, who on that 16 June had got up alongside the police chiefs and pleaded for an end to the madness, had been freshly sentenced. Mandela was still in prison, fourteen years on. Steve Biko, his near-rival as leader of the Black Consciousness movement, had been martyred in police custody. The figures of authority were nearly all absent. It seemed a time for fighting.

I realised we had picked the wrong undercover vehicle this time. The Isuzu TW20 6x6 looked far too military, in fact it was a Japanese copy of a US army truck. In some other place perhaps, yes—but not Soweto. As I had driven towards the township the only other vehicles in sight were the SADF carriers, as though armour awaiting other armour on a battlefield. But past them I could see the smoke, the burning rubbish, the open-air cooking fires, and it seemed a signal. I was determined. I had not shaved for days, like a soldier trying to be as thickskinned as possible. I was wearing an old torn jacket and braces, the farmer-guise, complete with a pitchfork beside me in the seat. I should have had a widebrimmed farmer's hat but I had lost it. But I had made sure my Makarov pistol was on me, wedged into the small of my back at the waistband and fully cocked. I was doing my own thing.

As a key logistics officer I should have been cleverer but the atmosphere of the area had got to me. I knew Soweto well. I had pastored here in the sixties, keeping in touch with Transkeian folk day-working in Johannesburg. I had held services here. I had met Winnie Mandela many times. I knew the Mandela home on Orlando West, one of the main Soweto streets. I knew most of the other streets too—Zola, Dube, Dobsonville, Zoni—but I was some way away. I was driving along Meadowland East from the direction of Johannesburg and passing more carriers and Landrovers. The softtop had been rolled back. It was the first time I had been here since the shootings and I found myself transfixed. It had never been a pretty place—what township was?—but it slowly assembled itself to me like a scene from Hell. I had flashes of Goya and old religious paintings. Odessa the Russian hero-city had lasted 69 days under siege before falling. The Soweto siege was hundreds of days on and if an onslaught came there had to be some defence. Other guns were in there of course but under the 'M' plan no street could be sure if the neighbouring street was ready. The bigger the stockpile, the better.

Maybe I had fooled myself into thinking I was nearly invisible, that the Boers were used to big trucks laden with market produce, but I was quite shocked when three panzer-like shapes swung onto Meadowland and blocked me off, with a fourth behind.

At first I didn't believe it. I was going through a thick bank of smoke and ash, the stuff was whitening my bonnet and screen and I had even used the washer-wiper. And then these Buffalos were suddenly waiting. High up on their backs were helmeted men with rifles and they were into the aim. They all seemed ghostly and unreal at first and the smoke seemed even thicker. I made out strained faces under the helmets. All were in flakjackets. Several were black. In the smoke our vehicles all looked similar, their khaki paintwork almost the same as my jungle-green. And green had been too armyish anyway. The smoke seemed to put everything in slow-motion. I squirted the screen ahead to get a clearer picture of the carriers. There was no hope of smashing through those things. They were a wall. One of the Buffalo front hatches opened.

The Isuzu had four forward gears but I couldn't remember which one I was in. I stalled—for the first time in years I stalled. A capped officer—a major—appeared with a shotgun in one hand, an automatic shotgun it looked like. He leant against a large lashed tyre which had been put there not only as a spare but to absorb sniper's bullets. He gripped the tyre and dropped to the ground. He started marching forward grimly, wreathed in smoke. He looked whiter than white for some reason. His shotgun was lowered as he came for my running board to close and question me and ask about my load. I coughed in the smoke. He'd turn and yell to a section to double and go through the vegetables and then find the AKs. I got ready as though in slow motion. I kept the engine stalled—there would never be any point starting up again. I leant forward to pull out my Makarov and start. I would take the officer and maybe two more on each Hippo before they reacted. Maybe I could empty the whole magazine and even have a go with the pitchfork by me, using it like some classic tribesman before the Brownings opened up.

The Makarov got caught a moment on my waistband but I knew it was free just as the major's foot came onto the running board and rocked the pickup with his weight. His face appeared, again whiter than white and he stared down hard. I was still bent over the wheel, hand to the small of my back. He stared at me hard, retched in the smoke, looked back at his vehicles and then growled angrily. He was about my age.

'Ach, kay mar, ol' da,' he said to me. 'Oh, just get going, pop.'

Those were the exact words he said to me. I'll never forget them. The next sounds were the revving of the Buffalos as he waved them back and slowly joined them without even taking a look at my load. Then my windscreen was emptying and the vehicles were on the hard shoulders, letting me through. I was still bent, one hand on my spine, disbelieving.

I did believe it, later. This was after I had rolled into Soweto and driven on to . . . I think the address was on Mfolo but I can't remember. I was in a daze long after the smoke cleared and I couldn't believe it. But as the AKs were quickly unloaded by anxious Sowetans, still wrapped in leaves in case informants were watching, I looked in my driving mirror for the first time . . . to see I was whiter than white for once. My hair and my beard looked grey if not snowy. I looked far older than forty-three. The smoke and ash, I realised, must have coated me through the open roof. Perhaps my bent posture had added to the wizened look that the major had taken in. I forgave him the insult to my vanity. His intelligence sources probably stated categorically that *Umkhonto we Sizwe* were not yet recruiting pensioners into their ranks. That major would have been off-duty when I drove out of Soweto later, nothing incriminating on the truck now and even the Makarov left behind as part of the town's arsenal, and I was glad. Though I took a razor to my chin soon after, the shave I got was nowhere near as close.

13

Namibia

The effects of that daring Boer raid on the SWAPO bases deep inside Angola were still being felt months later; the supply lines across the Namibian border had still not been repaired. The SWAPO groups inside Namibia itself were out on a limb. Not only were they short of supplies but, more dangerously, their morale had ebbed, which was leading to desertions and defections. But there was no way to reach them. New trails from other Frontline states like Botswana and Zambia had been quickly jumped on.

As I said earlier, SWAPO had turned to the *Umkhonto* for help and a brand-new trail had been hit upon, one that matched the best of Boer audacity. It was to reach those groups from the south, by coming right up through Namibia from the Cape itself. It would be a thousand-mile journey, equivalent to the length of Britain or a drive from San Francisco to the Canadian border, or the distance they had driven a dying Steve Biko to get treatment. A drive it would be indeed, with just one man and one vehicle expertly camouflaged. As I said, the guy centre-stage was me.

The vehicle was purchased at a garage near the Cape, for cash. The cash was from ANC funds smuggled in by a girl courier, always the most trustworthy. By now myself back in the same area, I was handed the keys. I stared hard at my operations vehicle, and it was worth staring at. It was the very reverse of the scruffy workhorses I had used before on smuggling runs. It was probably one of the best cars in the world. It was a BMW 725 saloon finished in metallic-grey. It was sheer luxury. The luxuriousness and the aura of privilege were to be part of the camouflage.

My cover was that of a successful travelling salesman. With more funds in my pocket, I went to one of Cape Town's top tailoring shops and bought two of the very best suits. The proprietor was an Asian whose attitude when he saw the colour of my skin changed when he saw the colour of my money. I chose carefully. One suit would be British-style pinstripe as close to Savile Row as possible, while the other would be Italian-American cut. It felt bizarre, to be buttoning up a waistcoat before a mirror, when a few weeks before I had been in filthy camouflage overalls in a jungle camp. I felt like an actor. I had my hair carefully cut, and a manicure, all to look the part, to stand up to close inspection. The shirts I bought were all high-collared, to hide the marks of AK-47 slings on my neck. I bought a box of cigars, Canary-Islands rather than Havanas which were of course officially unavailable in South Africa.

At a job lot I purchased a mass of IBM computer tapes. There were two reasons for this; one, it was such new technology that very few people in this part of the world would know much about it and could challenge my cover, and two, I could easily intermingle detonators and stripped-down pistols with the tapes. Other weapons and supplies I carefully cached inside and underneath the car, using a welding-torch on one occasion. I suppose the closest the whole notion came to was that guy Ian Fleming's ostentatious smuggler Goldfinger, though with my build I probably looked more like his henchman Oddjob. I checked a roadmap for my route. My destination was to be a town called Oshakati, one of the closest to the Angola border. That was where the SWAPO cell was based. To get there I would have to pass thousands of Boer occupation troops the length of Namibia. To crown it all, Oshakati itself was also the actual SADF Operational Headquarters and would be swarming. It promised to be some 'crossing'.

There were quite a few BMWs in Cape Town but none I think with a black driver, although few busy city people noticed. On the northern outskirts I got more looks. I took out a cigar and used my teeth on it as I had seen the Cubans do in Angola, letting the automatic gears do the work. More people stared, blacks and whites as I purred past. I stopped for a moment to look out at Robben Island and got steeled by the sight. I remembered to drop the hard look though and the cigar kept my smile fixed. I drove due north on the road for Springbok, Namaqualand and the Namibian border. The BMW and I got more looks from all races. My codename should, I decided, have been changed to 'Zilibanze' or rich guy. I settled in the seat, a living and moving example of black enterprise. How many Irish people there are among the whites of South Africa I never knew, but any of them seeing me that day would have said that, to be sure, *there* was a guy living the life of Riley.

Pretoria had long tried to sell the image of successful blacks within apartheid, frequently jetting such people to the States and Western Europe to show them off, and some Boers themselves had even begun to believe it. The propaganda seemed thankfully to be working for me as I began to encounter police and military vehicles, and simply got grins or admiring glances rather than suspicious stares. At one level, then, I knew I was passing muster. My route was one of the best in all southern Africa, due north and fairly straight, which allowed me to look in my mirror. I kept looking. To other drivers it probably appeared vain, a flashy black guy checking to see how fine he looked, but I was checking to see if I was being followed.

Two elements I knew could be on my tail. One

was South African Security Branch. Independent of ordinary police or army, they could be playing the same sophisticated game I was and following all the way to finally nail my SWAPO contacts. An informer or defector could have told them plenty. Secondly, I could have ANC itself behind, a commissar checking my movements. On numerous occasions, guerrillas on a mission had absconded with funds and enforcers had been brought in. There might also be ANC ahead at the side of the road, prewarned to watch out for me and report my progress. They couldn't miss me, that was for sure.

Though I had no devious plans I kept watching the mirror, although it was difficult in the glare and the road was coursing west with the sun. Several times a fast car came up and sat for a while. Although the 725 had the power to leave anything standing I knew not to risk speeding. I allowed myself to be overtaken by other smirking salesmen. There was still the risk of a clever front tail, a Security Brancher watching his mirror for me, but I had discounted that within an hour or so. I tried to relax and selected a tape—the *Eroica* by Beethoven, or 'van Beethoven' as my Gentleman farmer had called him. It was stirring stuff, with a hovering aspect to it. A moment later I stopped the car on a slope and looked back at the sky for signs of a distant helicopter. I remembered that Alouette over the Kalahari. There was nobody trailing from the air. I started up again. The same Kalahari was on my right, stretching hundreds of miles, but I would soon be crossing another desert, the Namib the land ahead was called after.

I decided to stay in South Africa the first night and stopped at a three-star hotel in Springbok. My drive was to be leisurely and almost ridiculously pampered. The car, the suit and the sight of a hefty tip caused any racial barriers to evaporate at the hotel. I got a good room and washed and changed, again laughing at my spartan existence in bush camps a few weeks before. I went down for a meal, but though I sat back I didn't drop my guard. The waiters, though black, could also be in touch with local police and if I made a mistake through ignorance my cover would be blown skyhigh. I decided to order a French dish and did such a good job of the pronunciation that a nearby white couple toasted me. That was new; I had of course only been *grilled* by Boers before.

I swanked back to the hotel room, but almost made a blunder. It had a television set—South African Broadcasting had only very recently started the new service—and I was unused to the controls. A porter entered, saw me and adjusted a knob. I realised a supposed technocrat like me should have found volume no problem. In fact I knew how to assemble the latest Soviet army radios, but television—no. I saw a curious look in the porter's eye which I hoped a generous tip would handle. I watched some American Western with Afrikaans subtitles and went to sleep.

The knock on the door made me jump and I
had visions of police and dogs. It was the porter
with morning coffee and my late call. I had a late
breakfast and it was well after nine when I left,
having checked nobody had touched the BMW
overnight. In my mirror I saw two black hotel staff
stare, but only surely with envy or admiration. I
drove sedately on into the best of the day and
reached the Namibian border within the hour.
Boer ideas helped me along. Namibia was regarded as South West Africa, part of the Republic's
territory, so there was no border check, though I
saw the usual clutch of Landrovers and Casspirs as
I crossed the natural frontier, the Orange River
bridge.

Now the scenery was no longer semi-desert but
true desolation. Canyonlands had begun. And
over some canyons I saw two helicopters keeping
abreast. I swallowed and put the *Eroica* back on
rewinding to the first movement, the most sooth-
ing. Only when the tape ended did I notice the sky
was clear. They had probably been heading for the
coast, for Luderitz. I decided to run Handel's
Water Music.

At Keetmanshoop I stopped to water myself. I
noticed much more military traffic, not only personnel carriers but tank-transporters. You could
tell which ones had come from the north by the
thick film of dust. The BMW would soon lose its
shine. It still got looks as I continued north but my
own glances went to the dune country, the real

Namib. I looked at my watch and realised I had lost time. I wanted to be in a hotel long before nightfall. The BMW was a broad-daylight car and might attract the wrong attention by dark. I speeded up. A few minutes later I swore as a motorcyclist appeared in my mirror.

I had been just over the limit, just. I stuck another cigar in my mouth and got ready to slow and smile winningly but there was no need. It was not a speedcop but an army despatch-rider who came abreast and then tore past. His dust covered more of the 725's paintwork.

I arrived in Windhoek, the Namibian capital, just before dusk and found the three-star hotel I was after. The place was full of South African soldiers, but many of them were black. I could feel the first tension now; the Namibia I had passed through had been a backwater but now it was SWAPO country. There had been incidents here in Windhoek, I knew. The leader of the Hereros, one of the main tribes, had been gunned down in a nearby street less than six months before. His killers had been SWAPO, who recruited mainly from the rival Ovambos; as usual everywhere in Africa, the tribal element was still to the fore.

As I sat having a meal of sausage and beer, a leftover from the days when Namibia had been a colony of the Kaiser's Germany, I considered my next movements. I was sure no one was shadowing me, but the further north I headed the more dangerous it was, with SWAPO itself the greatest threat. Only the cell in Oshakati knew a supply-run was coming while other groups, with commu-nications largely cut, knew nothing. They had been going for soft targets like local leading blacks, headmen, politicians and businessmen, and nobody looked juicier than me in my German car. Not even its excellent construction would stop a T76 landmine or a HEAT rocket.

I slept badly that night despite the superb room. I kept feeling the Makarov under my pillow. My body felt stiff after the previous day behind the wheel. As I had breakfast, I noticed two men in civilian clothes near the BMW. They were white. They could have been admiring the bodywork or perhaps they were gauging the weight by the wheels. I was sure this time it was Security Branch. The possibility had been discussed during planning at SWAPO. It had been suggested I booby-trap the car but I had objected. If my cover was blown I was to abandon the BMW and disap-pear on foot for the nearest public transport. At least here in Windhoek there were plenty of escape routes, even an international airport. I took ano-ther look at the pair and was still unable to decide if they were car enthusiasts or police. I decided not to panic. I went for a stroll round town.

It was quite pleasant with definitely German rather than Ango-Dutch architecture. There was a market nearby and I bought some local trinkets including a miniature Bushman's bow. Most of the blacks here were tall in stature, far taller than me, reflecting their rangy lifestyle. I saw many tall guys in Boer uniform complete with soft hats, and always armed with FN-style rifles. Souvenirs in my hand, I hailed a taxi and was ignored by two drivers. The third stopped, seeing the money in my hand, and I ordered him back to the hotel. The BMW was standing on the carpark alone with no sign of watchers, but it looked dusty and crest-fallen. I looked at my Bushman bow and tried to be brave. I ordered the taxi to halt, paid my fare and returned to my hotel. There were no strange looks, I thought, so nobody had been in asking questions. I took a deep breath and requested someone to wash my car for next morning as I was headed north. The white receptionist nodded and made a note. I waited on the nearby stairs to check if he made a phone call but two guests appeared to take his attention. I had an early meal, this time Italian not German, and took a large brandy. It was either that or the previous night's restlessness which this time helped me get a good night's sleep.

I awoke with the sun already drenching the room and looked out to see a black boy lathering the BMW from end to end. It looked respectable again. He was still busy washing when I dressed in my pinstripe and went to breakfast. It didn't occur to me that I must have had a funereal look. From the table I saw a local white with fruit, obviously a farmer, staring at the car. He looked disgusted.

'*Gut wasser,*' I heard him say, complaining at

170

such waste in this arid place.

'*Gut auto von Bayern,*' I heard another voice say.
Good Bavarian car. I did a doubletake. It was one
of the jerkined men of the day before. He was
either a BMW fanatic or one cool cop. I tried to
match his coolness when I checked out with him
hanging around, although I was sweltering in the
pinstripe. It felt like a uniform of defiance though.
Knowing I was being watched I swanned out
behind my portered bags.

'*Mein herr,*' that same voice said.

I turned to find the two young jerkined men
grinning, one aiming at me. I slowly lowered my
gaze. It was my Bushman bow.

I thanked them, stowed my possessions and
drove out, using the wipers on the screen. They
were still watching. I fumbled for a tape and
found the *Pastoral,* pushed in the nearby cigar-
lighter and slid out into the main street. I studied
the map as I drove and decided to make a detour
from the main route just in case. At Okahandia, I
turned onto a lesser road for a town called Karbib
and then continued north. This time there was
increased military traffic, but this was already a
main road running into Walvis Bay, the giant
enclave which had been South African even in the
Kaiser's time. My mirror stayed empty.

I drove on with more Beethoven and found
another sight to stare at as three-thousand-metre
Mount Etjo thrust up. At Otijiwarongo I regained
the main road and waited for more army convoys

to pass. There would be nonstop military stuff all the way to the border area now. I stayed behind a truck full of soldiers for half an hour. They looked very young and were probably national servicemen but two of them looked very like the jerkined pair back in Windhoek. Surely not. They could not be that smart. I followed the convoy across the Etosha Pan and saw two cheetahs. One of the truck soldiers raised his rifle at the beasts but two comrades disarmed him. I gave one a smile. Then their faces about-turned to the north.

We were now in Ovamboland, real bandit country, and I could see signs of war—barbed-wire fences, burnt-out trucks, blacks with preoccupied faces. The town of Tsumeb came and went. The countryside was getting flatter, drier and I was reminded of Angola which of course was the same terrain but separated by an old colonial border. More *Olifant* tanks appeared, guns facing north but the crews looked relaxed. Their May raids had of course solved a lot of problems. Certainly though I saw more burnt-out trucks they seemed to have been lying there for many months.

And then suddenly I was approaching Oshakati and the army drivers were pulling off. It looked a small shanty-style town and I found myself trying to remember the address. It was a number on the main street, which looked like the only street. I suddenly realised how incongruous the car looked set against this. There were no other civilian cars in sight, just a few trucks. I would have to stop and knock on doors. And then from an alley came a wild figure, another rangy Namibian. He flung himself at the door though it was locked. He tried to speak. I lowered the window an inch.

'Comrade Miwe,' he breathed in English.

I let him in and we drove out of town, past two Casspirs and I found I was back on the approach-road and passing the same burnt-out trucks. At the second truck however, my SWAPO contact leapt out and whistled. I heard an answer. Two distant figures appeared either side, obvious look-outs. My contact pointed down. I realised that there was a deep deliberately-dug pit under the truck. This was the cache. I had used similar stunts before, utilising previously-raided caches. This was the same idea. The burnt-out truck was part of the scenery, passed by Boers every day, but also a handy landmark. I helped quickly unload my supplies and in five minutes the BMW had a totally innocent cargo. Then I was off and returning to Oshakati. I knew what to say. I went straight to the police station and asked to see the officer-in-charge.

He had a Cape accent and he looked hot and bothered.

'What do you want, *mynheer*?'

I nodded to the sound of typewriters. 'I represent IBM, sir,' I said. 'We could revolutionise your office system.'

173

'Not today thank you, *mynheer.*'

'But I have equipment of the eighties here, sir. Your office work will be so much easier.'

'I said not today, thank you.'

'But I've come a long way.'

'Not today. We are busy.'

A black policeman yelled over. 'Sergeant, the Inspector on the phone.'

The white policeman looked back at me. 'Sorry, we're busy today.'

'Could I call again?'

The sergeant was already marching away. *'Ja,* if you like, whatever.' I took that as an invitation. I drove out of Oshakati and retraced my route through Windhoek, staying at the same three-star hotel and informing them I would be passing through again. I did, on four more occasions, traversing Namibia from north to south in the same luxury car. The BMW publicity called it the 'Ultimate Driving Machine'. I didn't know it, but that fifth trip would be *my* ultimate drive. Although I would carry out a few more infiltrations on foot, my crossing days were now numbered.

14

Lesotho

Lesotho, another independent country, was another of our boltholes, but it had one big drawback. Totally surrounded by South Africa, it was an island set high and dry on land. Like Botswana to the north, the borders were closely watched, but with a land area of only just over ten thousand square miles, Lesotho was a much easier job. It was the old Basutoland, a largely mountainous kingdom which had been the place where the Basotho tribe had made a last stand against the Boers and then, defeated, had placed itself under British protection so their enemies would never come back. Yet in the twentieth century they, like most of the Frontline states, were also dependent on South African trade, so the Premier, Chief Jonathan, ran a balancing act. Many of his people had to cross the border for work in places like the Rand goldfields.

A 'goldworker' was one of my disguises when I mingled with returning Basothos. The main border crossing was the Maseru bridge that led to the capital. On other occasions I would wear herder's clothes, sometimes a straw Basotho hat and sometimes local tribal costume. Once with a police Landrover on watch I pretended to be a shepherd, though my background was of course cattle. The sheep knew too, but my amateurishness only got guffaws. Once in the country, an *Umkhonto* guy did one of two things. He reported in to the ANC offices and rested before returning to South Africa some way or another, or he stepping-stoned to a proper Frontline state.

This meant going by air. The catch of course was that any plane leaving Lesotho entered South African airspace and could not continue on a direct flight to its destination. It was obliged to land at a South African airport for inspection. It was of course an outrage, but with one of the most formidable airforces on the continent, Pretoria called the tune. One was obliged to go through a second customs check, passport irregularities were pounced upon and many an air traveller got no further.

It was not a problem for ANC guys though, with passports furnished by the United Nations which amounted to diplomatic immunity. Touchdown airports or not, no UN passport holder could be touched. We knew it, and the Boers knew it. But dirty tricks could be employed. One was deliberately getting the precious passport mislaid. A hired pickpocket could do the job and suddenly a guy was totally vulnerable on South African soil.

Another was close surveillance of passengers when they made their temporary landing, to record who was who.

I remember a time when I had come to Maseru a harder way through a fence. I was headed for Lusaka and I had quickly been furnished with documentation. That same evening the jet had taken off and within a minute or so we were over hostile territory. I had clutched the passport tightly, watching out for any clever fingers, even from attractive black air hostesses who could be Security Branch agents, and then we headed in to land for Boer inspection. A Mirage circled as our jet landed in Natal. The hatch opened and the passengers filed out one by one. I was about tenth off and I started down the steps, only to notice a guy in mechanic's overalls aiming a camera and taking shots of everyone. I knew my face was known so I engineered a diversion. As he was focusing on me I pretended to stumble down the flight steps. I think he missed getting my face. I was wearing the collar and all.

I smiled as my passport was grudgingly checked and then our plane was cleared for takeoff with no passengers taken off.

The smile was still on my face as we came into Lusaka. I did not realise that it would soon be wiped off completely. I wouldn't just stumble. I was headed for the biggest-ever fall.

15

Rhodesia

*T*he ten-man guerrilla groups were ideal for southern Africa. A section or squad of guys moving through the bush could just about keep their presence a secret. Any larger-sized unit living rough would very quickly be noticed. The game would be given away by game itself. The opposition knew that to watch for men you first kept an eye on the wildlife.

We learnt that the hard way in Rhodesia.

In 1977 a company-sized ZIPRA group had infiltrated the Rhodesian border from the southwest, from Botswana. Ninety guerrillas intended to attack targets in Bulawayo, the country's second city. The men were mainly of the Matabele tribe, operating in their own natural territory, but someone should have known better. They were detected first by the wildlife which fled accordingly at their approach. Soon the creatures were becoming unevenly distributed in the area. When the guerrillas reached Matopos National Park, bigger creatures moved away from their usual trails. A park ranger quickly noticed and guessed the reason. Within hours the Rhodesian army and airforce were closing in. All ninety ZIPRA were accounted for. The predatory wildlife when it returned to the area would have been excited by the traces of blood. This was why, some time later when ANC made that Limpopo crossing, we went ten at a time, though even then it might have been disturbed wildlife that led to the ambush of the second wave.

For Rhodesia, which bore a far closer resemblance to the South African bush than either Angola or Namibia, was the real hunting country. If Zambia was like a lion, then Rhodesia was the lioness, the real killer. Some strategists saw it as a microcosm of South Africa and therefore the ideal site for blooding ANC cadres. Ben Bella the Algerian leader had once stated at an OAU conference that you should take out the weakest first. Rhodesia was a much weaker, smaller country than South Africa, but it had a similar background of white supremacy so our interest was obvious, which is why we had so much to do with the Patriotic Front groups.

I myself only went into Rhodesia three times, the first being en route to that Limpopo ford in camouflage suit with civilian clothes beneath.

The second time I began in civilian clothes. I was posing as a townsman in the capital Salisbury. I had gone there to help lead out a batch of new recruits for the Patriotic Front. As far as white

Rhodesians were concerned I was one of *their* blacks. I could speak the local Ndbele language. I remember taking in a lot of Salisbury as I walked through the streets. There was so much Britishness about the place and I was reminded of my London days. There were various reminders of Churchill and there was a Woolworths, though that had been bombed by ZANLA some months before. There was also an Americanness. I noticed a police unit on patrol which looked very similar to a New York SWAT team. A cinema near Cecil Square had just premiered the latest Hollywood epic *Star Wars*. The film's story of valiant rebels facing an enemy led by a guy with an obvious black voice was probably much appreciated. Another part of the film— I actually saw it years later—was in fact a joke on them. A major hideout was based in ancient ruins, and for black nationalists there really *was* such a place.

The Great Zimbabwe ruins to the south of Salisbury was used by us, and in fact when I picked up my nine black recruits from the city, that was where I took them, with camouflage suits waiting. The ruins were a major rendezvous spot for guerrilla groups. Though the Rhodesian security forces made raids and stakeouts, the ruins with their walls and enclosures which were once a city-state would have required whole brigades to render them secure, and Rhodesians did not have that manpower. In fact, white manpower was their greatest weakness and the Rhodesians couldn't keep stretching it year after year. They had begun their real mobilisation in 1972 and the use of so many men plus the various UN sanctions was slowly but surely bleeding the Smith government dry. It didn't need a trained economist like me to see that.

But during my time there the Rhodesians' blood was right up. They were clawing in all directions. Not only had they hit camps in Zambia, Mozambique and Botswana but, obviously still very much in collusion with Pretoria, they were hitting Namibia's Caprivi Strip. They actually once reached one thousand kilometres into Angola. Furthermore, like the Boers, the Rhodesians were good, too good, and guerrillas in their ten-man groups usually avoided contact if possible in time-honoured tradition. All the same, sometimes there was nowhere to run, and by 1978 there had been over three thousand casualties among ZANLA, ZIPRA and ANC compared with under three hundred of the Security Forces. I was around though, when there came a moment to even the odds that same year.

It happened up on the Zambezi River, bordering Zambia, though this time I was firmly on Rhodesian soil. We were in one of the few sectors where all the Patriotic Front were co-operating properly. We were all in camouflage, even Mugabe's normally-ragtag ZANLA men, and based at a secret camp, when a runner brought

sensational news. Nearby, on the Zambezi itself, a
unit of Rhodesian soldiers had gone off-duty for
the day and were swimming in the river. The unit
were all white. That meant it could be one of two
units, 1st Rhodesian Light Infantry or SAS. All
other units, even the counter-guerrilla 'Selous
Scouts', were integrated. But along with the
Scouts, RLI and SAS were our most dangerous
opponents, and it appeared we had been presented
with an opportunity of giving them a taste of their
own medicine. Another runner came with a fresh
report. The bathing soldiers were being guarded
by black troops, probably men of the so-called
Guard Force, a unit raised in a protector role
throughout Rhodesia.

We planned fast. For once ZANLA and ZIPRA
officers forgot differences. Speed was of the
essence. We were five miles from the bathing spot
and would have to get there on foot. We would
overpower the black guards, then open up on the
whites in the water. It would be a simple hit, the
sort of thing their special forces had done countless
times to our camps. Within thirty minutes, things
were under way, but it was not to be a mad charge
to the killing ground. We had learnt lessons.
Again, a mass movement would disturb wildlife
and give out early warnings. Tripwires might have
been laid. A first wave was despatched, these
being ZIPRA men who were local. They knew the
area and would also be of the same tribe as the
riverside guards. They would get close enough to

disarm or dispatch them. The second wave to leave five minutes later were mainly ZANLA. A composite group including ANC guys made up the third.

I can remember taking off at a fast trot, my AK in my hands and hundreds of rounds of extra ammo weighing me down. We had all loaded up for maximum firepower. The actual physical effort of a battle march with this load kept my mind focused, the exhilaration of going into battle proper for the very first time filling me. And then suddenly we could glimpse water through the trees and a ZIPRA man was waving us down, his eyes white with excitement. We were a hundred yards from the river. The first wave had taken the guards, killing some and capturing others. I glimpsed a group of prone men in khaki uniform being covered by some ZANLA to my right. They were bareheaded and I presumed the first-wave men were wearing their bush hats to keep up the element of surprise. As we crawled forward I could see the second wave moving ahead, some lugging heavy machine guns to make a real massacre. For the next few minutes as we crawled my emotions were those of a stalking hunter after a man-eater, a combination of excitement and vindictiveness.

And then I heard a distant sound. It was a transistor radio. One of those white swimmers was playing music to add to the holiday atmosphere. I have since tried to identify it and I think it was the tape of *Saturday Night Fever*.

The disco track got louder as my group crawled on, though all I could see was the backs of ZANLA men as they slid forward and there was just a glimpse of water through the trees. But the river bank could only be about fifty yards away now. I could already imagine the scene; some white guys would be actually swimming, despite the bilharzia risks, and some would be sunning themselves, drinking cans of beer, playing cards or reading, and all of them hearing that disco music I was hearing. The sandy shores of the Zambezi was the nearest thing to a real seaside beach.

Maybe it was the thought of real sandy beaches and my Wild Coast boyhood that triggered it, but suddenly I thought of my young days and then my Gentleman farmer. And the farmer's son, whom I hadn't seen since the early sixties. He would be in his forties like me, with maybe a son like me. The son would be around twenty. Military age. What if the boy had been called up into the South African army and as sons go, had opposed the old family liberalism and become a gung-ho soldier? What if he had volunteered for secondment to the Rhodesians, as many Boer boys had? What if he was one of those young men swimming beyond the trees? It was a ridiculous thought, I know, but the longer the moments ticked by, the stronger the image became. He would have the family looks, those light bright eyes. But white guys, those white guys by the lake especially, were the enemy and it was them or us. We crawled on. I passed a discarded piece of webbing which some guard had had taken off at gunpoint, but I could feel the heat in me dying by the second. The cold-bloodedness was now a different thing. I heard the radio change tune distantly and so did a hundred other guys. Some ZANLA officer took that as his cue.

I had just started to see the real blue of the river when all hell broke loose. Ahead of me AKs opened up and someone used a rifle grenade with an SKS. A heavy machine-gun started, one of our RPGs by the fire-rate. Through it I could hear that radio still blaring. Then a ZANLA officer appeared, bush hat on head and waved us forward with some Shona war-cry. The noise was now deafening as dozens of AKs fired. Still that radio was playing. My group tore forward to add our firepower. I had my gun ready as ahead of us the skyline clouded with gunbursts and leaping spent cartridges and the backs of crouched and kneeling guerrillas. I got one glimpse of the river, the sandy beach and smoke and one, two white bodies in bathing trunks. As I swivelled my gaze to look for targets there suddenly came a whoosh. Then the whole picture of the Zambezi flashed and shuddered. Our fire was being returned.

Somebody down there was using a mortar. Two guerrillas were sent flying. More blasts came, sending more guys reeling. Now I could hear new guns. FN machine guns. Some men down there had survived and were reacting. They would have their personal weapons to hand. I hadn't fired yet, though I saw one of my sergeants ahead emptying his AK. He too ducked as a new mortar round came in. Then three more came in as many seconds. Bits of tree started flying everywhere and I saw a guerrilla scream with a slashed face. I heard a shout, a white battle cry, an Anglo-Saxon swearword, and two ZIPRA men in bush hats came flying back. The men on the beach were counterattacking. Though nearly naked, they were coming right back at us. I saw a ZIPRA man point left, then right. They were coming on our flanks. Another mortar shell screamed in and a whole tree toppled. We ducked from the flailing bits of branch.

Now someone yelled retreat. Still I could hear that radio. There also came a familar sound. Helicopters. We had to go now. Around me guerrillas pulled back as more shells slammed around us. Now I could see we had casualties. Two men hopped past, their camouflage suits red. Another guerrilla staggered into view towards me. I ran to him, past him and saw white smoke everywhere, no glinting blue water in sight. Another mortar had laid down a covering screen. I could smell the phosphorus. Although I could see nothing, I aimed first left and then right, where the outflankers would be, and emptied my magazine, reloaded and emptied another. Then at a shout from a ZIPRA man I turned and fled from distant swearing and that mad radio.

We dispersed in thick bush due west of the

ambush, the groups of ten splitting into groups of three. Some tried to run for Zambia, others went for Botswana. We moved southwest, then northwest for the Victoria Falls. We made it. Both Botswana and Zambia were hit in reprisal raids by Rhodesian special forces within weeks.

No doubt there will be official records regarding the Zambezi ambush of off-duty soldiers. Whether they were SAS or RLI will also be on file, along with the toll of casualties of either side. It was an action lasting less than ten minutes but it was one of the longest days of my life. When my two guys and I rested that night I took first watch all through the small hours, knowing we would sit tight until scorching midday. Though I had the AK ready and was fully alert, I had a million whirling thoughts. Until a voice said, 'Comrade Miwe, it's a new day. I'll relieve you.' And was I relieved.

There were not too many days to go before the most devastating of ambushes was to be sprung on me.

16

Swaziland-Mozambique

$\mathcal{I}$t was the smallest of our boltholes and half the size of Lesotho, but Swaziland had been accorded the most modern Boer security precaution: a massive electrified fence. The fence ran north from the beginning of the Swazi border with Mozambique. Modelled on the French barrages constructed during their Algerian war to keep out terrorists and running for hundreds of kilometres, the voltage of the fence was more than enough to kill. Which it did, though for every human being, a hundred wild animals died. To run the wire the full length of the Mozambique-South Africa frontier would have been far too costly, so the barrier changed from the modern to the archaic.

Continuing the border security was no less an institution than the Kruger National Park. With literally thousands of animals and the biggest concentration of the 'Big Five' in South Africa, especially lions, cheetahs and rhinos, the park would be a near-suicidal place to cross on foot. The Boers were well aware of this. It was so dangerous that they used it as a final training-ground for their own special forces, sending troopers in to live rough for days or even weeks. The troopers would be armed, though. A guerrilla infiltrator might walk into one of them even if he had avoided the animals. If the white troopers themselves were attacked by beasts they could defend themselves and their shooting would be identifiable to friendly listeners. Guerrilla AK-47s would have produced a different reaction; like the Romans the Boers would have probably sent more lions in. There was yet another snare on the Mozambique side of the border, in the shape of RENAMO. This 'National Resistance Movement', which opposed the Mozambican President Samora Machel and his allies, operated as far south as Swaziland.

I needed to enter Swaziland though. A lot of *Umkhonto* officers did. A major ANC conference had been called in Mbabane the capital. The whole 'Unofficial Executive' was to be there—it couldn't be too official with the attention that would bring. But it was 1979, the threshold of a new decade and a look at future strategy was called for, plus a résumé of results so far. So the call had gone out, and guys were coming in from all directions, from Frontline states and from South Africa itself. Boer intelligence had got wind and they were out to intercept as many big fish as they could. Along the Mozambique border RENAMO became suddenly very active, making crossings difficult. But guys still got through. Some had to be escorted by

Machel's troops, some pretended to be RENAMO themselves to do it.

One tough guy came in through the electrified fence; one even tougher guy in through both the Kruger *and* that fence. I had done tough things for the cause but not on this occasion. I came into Swaziland's international airport, Manzini, from Mozambique, easy-as-pie on my UN passport. It was one of my simplest crossings ever. I left the passport at the ANC office in Mbabane and was in good time for the meeting.

There was a lot to talk about. I was in a smart suit, the same pinstripe I had bought for my Namibian 'crossings'. It was a shame to waste it and this after all was an important occasion. I met men of the High Command and Regional Command for the first time. It was weird, after those years through the seventies, working in cells, either in towns or guerrilla camps, and now I was meeting people. I suppose all of us had come a long way. It had really just been three years' service for me, but things were looking up in Rhodesia. Elections had finally been called. After nearly fifteen years of fighting the rebel government, despite the calibre of their soldiers, was almost on the ropes. In Namibia, South Africa was actually having talks with SWAPO. It seemed we were getting closer to home and we could plan a new strategy.

We now had a good few trained cadres on the ground, soldiers who were doing a civilian job but ready to drop everything if balloon-time came, just like the original Boer 'commandos' had done against the British a full century before. But though we had learnt a lot of skills working along-side the local guerrillas in Namibia and Rhodesia, South Africa was hardly a replica. As I pointed out to a tough guy commander who'd fought the Selous Scouts in Mozambique, the Boers could and would still make mincemeat of direct opposition. More Sowetos were just round the corner if we weren't careful.

While Pretoria had been losing in some areas, it had been gaining ground elsewhere. Its military supply was almost self-sufficient now; they produced all their own weapons and aircraft. Worst of all, they had produced the Bomb. With obvious Israeli help, they had tested a device way off the beaten track, in the Prince Edward Islands in the Indian Ocean. We all knew that a cornered animal was the most dangerous, that when you were about to win you could just as easily finally lose. There was a lot to thrash out.

In that room in that building in Mbabane, strategies were formulated. Some wanted urban terrorism. Others, like me, wanted soft supply targets like oil refineries. In Rhodesia the most devastating guerrilla strike had recently come about when ZANLA had rocketed the main oil-storage depot in Salisbury and destroyed nearly thirty per cent of the country's fuel supply. That was the way to do it, I was sure. Armed local insurrections which some guys were keen on would be destroyed piecemeal, just like the impis in the Zulu war. And Zulus were another problem; how to forge closer links with their tribal chiefs.

There was a lot of talk, but a lot of excitement. It was an historic meeting I suppose, even though it was highly unofficial with absolutely no photographs for obvious reasons. Then the Executive broke up and went its own way. I would go back into South Africa, which meant slipping in. I had no need of the UN passport, because I wasn't supposed to have been anywhere abroad, having never have been issued a passport by the Pretoria authorities. I took off my smart pinstripe and returned to Mozambique.

The country had a second, smaller and far more civilised border with South Africa, complete with long-established railway, though here too RENAMO helped check large-scale ANC infiltration. I was small-scale. At Ressano Garcia I boarded a southbound train with false papers. Without having encountered wild animals, electric wires or rebel Mozambicans, I went through the Boer border post and next morning I was in Johannesburg. Then I returned to Transkei and my home, my wife and kids, both of whom were now at the higher education stage.

I got a call a few nights later, to report to Umtata police station. I went along easily. A white officer was there and he looked senior.

'Just a few things, Mr Kobo,' he said.

193

'Sure, baas,' I replied, all smiles.

'Been anywhere recently?'

'Up north seeing a few friends, baas.'

'Okay, Mr Kobo.' He smiled affably and reached into a drawer. I wondered if he was getting me a drink. On my file my liking for brandy would be listed. He didn't take out a bottle. He took out a photograph, still smiling. He placed it on his desk and turned it. There I was, in my pinstripe, sitting among the Unofficial Executive of the ANC in that room in Mbabane. Someone in that room had taken a secret picture. All the faces had been checked against known photofiles and I had been identified.

The Boer officer was still smiling as the doors opened and four police came in. 'Been to Swaziland I see, Mister Kobo. Into the pit with your fellow snakes. You won't be going there or anywhere again. We've got three treason charges against you and each one carries the death sentence.'

These last few crossings had of course been far too easy.

His face became a snarling animal's.

'It's all over for you, man.'

17

The Mountain Prison

That distant snow-capped Drakensberg range that had for forty-five years been amongst my fondest dreams now became my worst nightmare. Those Dragon mountains were to Africans the 'Rampart of Spears'—*Quathlamba*—but both blacks and whites had usually been distant observers who rarely stayed for long.

For someone like me who would actually linger up there, and among perennially-snowy tracts, another name came up. The name was 'Kieskamahoek'. Translated from the Boer, it was half-tooth and half-hook. Its actual shape was neither sharp nor jagged but rectangular, squat and artificial. Kieskamahoek was the name of my new prison. In fact it was an old prison, for some time disused and then especially reopened for Joseph Kobo. No kidding. They had gone to a lot of trouble. They had installed new security precautions and enlisted a skeleton staff. I would never know exactly how many warders, but they were more than enough to handle one guy. It was to be total incommunicado. They knew all Joseph Kobo's tricks now, his turning cells into offices and running operations, subverting other prisoners and even guards. They knew the three years on Robben Island had only made him worse. He had three high-treason counts and maybe, thanks to the Swaziland informant, more was known. So someone senior had thought of a solution and remembered Kieskamahoek up in Joseph Kobo's mountains.

It was like a cruel joke, as though someone had deliberately tapped into my old memories. I might have talked about the Drakensberg when delirious, when under torture, but that of course was only coincidence. Total isolation in an isolated-enough region was careful objective thinking on someone's part all the same. I was obviously high on the public enemy list and though not a killer, I had supplied enough weaponry for there to be blood on my hands. Whether I had been seen as a Rudolf Hess-figure I don't know, but at obvious expense I was dispatched on a long truck journey out of the homelands.

Seated chained in the back between three guards, I felt the gradient slowly steepen and heard the driver change into lower and lower gear. It took hours. I was lashed to the vehicle itself and the guards used handholds in case someone was tossed over the tailboard. With a Landrover right behind, there was no chance of an en-route escape.

It was getting dark when we reached Kieskamahoek.

I soon learnt it would always be dark. The prison was in the lee of a South Drakensberg peak, which was why snow lay all year round, and why there was no real vegetation. There were no trees, no bushes, no grass; there was just snow and of course the grey of basalt and concrete. It was always cold. It didn't at first click when we arrived and I saw the guards in jackets and greatcoats. The Kieskamahoek warders were all black. With their thin African blood they were shivering, as I quickly did. But my teeth didn't chatter, for by now I had a gag.

The total-incommunicado regime was imposed straight away. The stillness was overwhelming, just like it had been that time in American snow but there, when other people had appeared, they had been brashly loudmouthed. Here they were all mutes. There was to be no verbal contact, not even monosyllabic formalities. All I heard was the crash of boots as I was marched to my cell. Other cells were left wide open as if to rub home the vindictiveness. Then it clanged shut. It would only open for mealtrays, and ablution cans. These were the only sounds, except for winds and an occasional lammergeyer bird. I didn't know how high I was. Obviously less than Mont-aux-Sources, the Dragons' ultimate three-thousand-metre peak, but my head took a while to adjust to the altitude.

Then I seemed to slow down. Things went into slow motion. It was as though I had landed on the moon. Alone. Except I was in thin prison garb. I shivered. I would fight to get warm, doing frenzied exercises to make sweat. But as I tired I would get all the colder, as though in icy water. The physical effort interfered with my thinking as the weeks marched into months.

It was now the eighties, I told myself, and things were progressing in South Africa. I tried to remember those big ANC talks on strategy. Exciting things were happening now Zimbabwe was won. The focus was on *Azania*, South Africa itself. I tried to tell myself this as I stared out of my small cell window at a world that was more Alpine than African. I was sure there would come a chink in the guards' armour, a chance to talk, form a friendship, and then have an enlisted helper. It had always happened before in the other prisons. But no chink came. The guards remained faceless and anonymous. The only other living thing I got to know was one big lammergeyer which became a frequent visitor, obviously attracted by the prison kitchen. I once watched it make its own meal, living up to its snake-vulture name by dropping a wriggling shape onto the rocks. But the bird's swoop was the only violent movement around me. Everything else was sanitised and in slow motion. My food was carefully cut to minimise the risk of choking, for nobody seemed to be having a close watch. I was being left to my own devices, but without any tools to work with.

I remembered my Russian training, tried to use my mind, to keep it active and committed. I kept my thoughts political. I worked out brand-new Ho Chi Minh trails across South Africa. I thought up new caching tricks. I wondered about Nelson Mandela. All through my *Umkhonto* years, even in far-off training camps, we had stressed the urgency of our struggle with the slogan: 'Hey guys, Rolihlahla will die if we don't keep on.' I didn't know what had happened. Was he still on Robben? Were there plans to rescue him finally regardless of his agreement? Was there a plan to rescue me in this eyrie?

Staring at the lammergeyer, I realised the bird was a clever killer, but it was a loner. I thought of all the guys I'd known in so many countries. After Rhodesia-Zimbabwe, if that had fallen, then the next were those under Boer control. Was there renewed fighting in Namibia? Were setpiece battles taking place in north Transvaal, or was there a sustained urban terrorist campaign? I shouted to the guards for news but there was no reply. I shouted in Xhosa, English, Afrikaans but there was no faltering in their steps as they marched away. I tried to insult them, swear at them—anything to provoke a reaction. I would have welcomed a bull-charge of angry men with fists and batons, but nobody came and my voice got hoarse with shouting.

I soon started speaking to myself. I had to keep

versed in all my languages. Not just the main South African tongues but the others I had picked up. Latin, Russian, the smattering of Arabic. My body got colder. I fashioned my pillow and blankets into a punchbag and threw swings and jabs for hours on end. I ran on the spot, covering hundreds of miles in my cell. As I jogged I thought of escape. The window was too small and too high but if I could get out that door for one split second, I could go like the wind and lose myself on the slopes, snow-covered or not. The door did not open. Even when I timed my whisper to the exact second of the arrival of my meal, informing the man outside that there was a ten-thousand-rand reward if only he would take a message to a friend.

The only friend I had was that vulturine bird which I watched making more and more kills a mile or so away. Sometimes, though, it would sail close to my window and for a while it formed part of a plan. If I could enlarge that window and be ready to grab the bird, it might carry me away or at least would break my fall. The image of such a notion seized me, furiously flapping bird being held by the claws despite a viciously pecking beak, and I worked on my window. I used my food knife. The concrete had been recently reset though. And the bird seemed to know. Even when I used precious crumbs of food tossed into the air, it kept its distance.

I thought of using the knife on the door, trying to locate a structural weakness. I thought of

literally strengthening my hand so that one day I
might smash through the door. All I did was open
the skin on my knuckles and nearly break my
wrist. My training had depended on human contact at some stage for escape and evasion. Here
they had thrown away the key. I would fly into a
rage at some point of each day at the waste of my
energy. I would curse the ANC for not mounting a
rescue. I cursed black guys, ANC and police. But
when I thought of Mandela it straightened things
out a little, for he would himself now be approaching his twentieth year in prison. Twenty years was
the sentence Mary Queen of Scots had endured
and Mandela had, I knew, often mentioned her
without identifying with her. But me and my
private prison were in some ways closer to her. I
remember laughing one day at the idea of a black
guy linked to a white queen, to any woman in fact.
And yet I was a married man with a family.

It was when two whole winters had come and
gone that I got my first real communication from a
guard as he brought my breakfast.

'By the way, Kobo.'

I almost dropped my plate. 'Yes? Yes?'

'A few months ago. Down in Transkei . . . '

'Yes, yes. What happened there? Tell me, tell
me.'

I heard his boot scrape slowly.

'Your wife died, Kobo.'

The plate fell on its own. The guard had
long gone when I began to function again. I

remembered my wedding. 1953, year of Everest. I felt the wind from outside. So much of my struggle had been for Angelinah. I had been trying to gain respect for us. Shape a new life other than the second-classness we and our forebears had known in our own land. And now this. I had left her to try and do something, left her in the care of our clan, and gone on those missions, those close shaves and I had survived. In peaceful pastoral Transkei, Angelinah had died. It was so unfair. I was the one who should have gone if anyone, and I was the bereaved.

I stopped looking for the lonely lammergeyer and the way it cruelly dashed living things. I stopped the punchbagging, the window-scraping. I sighed long, long sighs and began to slow down. I ate my main meal that night only because my stomach told me. I felt nothing pass the tightness in my throat and without the usual look around the mountains went straight to sleep like a young child.

Then I woke up to the new voice. It said, 'Joseph, why are you here?'

I blinked and reacted. The voice was not in Xhosa, which the guard had used earlier. Nor was it English or Afrikaans. It spoke again.

'Joseph, I called you to do a special thing. You don't need to be here. Why are you here?'

I gasped, grunted. What language was it I was hearing? I couldn't click and yet I knew every word. My eyes became one with the darkness.

There was no light anywhere and the door was shut with no sound beyond. There was just that mountain-stillness now. But it had to be a trick.

It had to be my guards, reinforced by Security Branch, using the latest technology. Hidden microphones, subliminal sound-effects, hypnosis, hallucinogens. I knew some of the tricks from Russian training . . . The voice had sounded so gentle yet so strong. I still didn't know what tongue it had used and yet the words had touched me deep inside, deeper than I had known for years.

Were Security Branch now that smart, that subtle? They must be, I reckoned. It certainly wasn't my imagination for I had felt the words carry across my cell and ring in the freezing air. It had been a voice all right, and some very clever guy, probably a white.

Otherwise, it would have meant that . . . that . . . I swallowed as I thought it. That God had come into my cell.

I looked around at the four dark corners. No. That was imagination, or madness, to think what it meant. It would come down to this. That the very year after my wedding when I had made a promise, it had been remembered. Which would mean that throughout all those later years, the two decades of doing my thing, activist to guerrilla, all across Africa serving the Military Wing, He had been waiting.

18

He Who Crosses Over

'You know why I am here,' I replied. I don't remember if I used English or Xhosa, but I spoke aloud in my cell, so that a close-at-hand listener would hear. I was over seventy per cent sure it was a Security Branch stunt. Now at least I had a chance to influence someone, especially if black guys were also in earshot. I continued. 'You know I've landed in this vile place because of my people being so oppressed. You know I'm fighting for their freedom. What else can I do? What else could I do these past twenty years as things got worse? This is what I had to do, become a fighter. Someone had to do it, to stand up to them.'

And then I heard that voice again, so powerful and so soft at the same time. 'This is not what I called you for, Joseph,' it repeated. 'Why are you here?'

That seventy per cent calculation blew apart in my head just then and I knew.

But by the next night I had managed to shake that knowledge off. I was able to make my earlier reply when I was spoken to again. And again. Every night, long after supper and lights out, when there was no other sound but wind, I was asked the same thing. Weeks became months and the voice kept coming. It was the same one. I knew beyond a doubt it could not be the same man, or even the same clever tape outside the cell. Nobody was outside. It took nearly three months, ninety nights of it, and then I broke down in tears.

I stuffed my mouth with my blanket but the blanket became soaked. I have never, never cried like that. My tears burned my face. My cheeks ballooned. It was as though I'd been plunged underwater. Those guys that had known me as a tough guy, brawler or guerrilla leader, they would have been mortified or filled with contempt. I didn't care about any other guys. I cried on and on and on, through days and through meals, the plates sliding in my wet fingers. I thought I'd never stop. All day and night it went on. It's the truth. The ducts did not dry up. My body heaved and heaved. I was on the floor when I looked up and blinked. I could go on like this for years, I would go on. There was all the time in the world. He had all the time. He was still waiting.

I swallowed hard and nodded and found the word. 'Lord, if you want me to serve you again . . . OK.'

I stopped crying that night and fell asleep.

When I woke up the breakfast tray was there and long cold. But I smiled. I had such a sense of peace and warmth. It was a cold morning but I didn't feel it. There was this inner glowing, like guys get when they know they are in love, but more than that. I ate my cold breakfast and it was delicious. The sky through the cell window was vivid blue with not a cloud. Yet it looked different up there.

It was different down here too. The new things started happening in Kieskamahoek prison within days.

First the grille stayed open and I saw a guard's face. He was black like me and not unlike me; despite his uniform it was like staring in a mirror. Then next day the door opened and he was there. He didn't have a mealtray for once. He spoke in Xhosa.

'Er . . . Mister Kobo, can I ask you something?' He had a pleasant voice but it was nothing like that voice I now knew so well. I smiled back, taking in his cap with the prison-service badge.

'Sure,' I smiled. Had he heard something these past weeks? He looked urgent.

'I understand you got a degree in economics once.'

I laughed. My face was back to normal size, but it seemed to be set in a grin. 'Sure. In London, England, it was.'

'Well, Mister Kobo. We're not well paid, our service. But . . . '

'Sure.'

'Well, I put some money aside though and I got

this insurance policy for when I retire and, well, I wonder if you could advise me about what to do.'

'OK. Let me see the policy,' I said to the guy who I could see was alone. 'And why not call me Joseph?'

The guard nodded. 'And I'm Michael.'

I sorted Michael's policy that same day, in time for it to be sent out with the mail, a service I had never been allowed to use. Next day another guard appeared, a guy named David. He was leaving the service to start up in a business with relatives. He needed advice. He had papers and estimates. He came into the cell and sat down. Another guard came with another problem, and then Michael came back to check something. I smiled at all of them. I knew they knew nothing about my change. I realised I was suddenly in an office again, though this time more an advice bureau. Despite their privileged occupation, they had an awful lot of personal problems. Maybe it was because of that occupation. But I found myself able to help. Whether it was loneliness at the remote posting, finances or woman-problems, I found myself effortlessly guiding. Kieskamahoek prison suddenly got noise for the first time. Guys started laughing. Maybe the laughter echoed in the mountains and got that lammergeyer into a flap.

It was David who came flying into my cell a week later with a worried look. 'You've got to pack all your things, Joseph. Quick.'

Two new guards came in right behind, black but hardfaced. 'We've come to take you back to Headquarters, Kobo.'

And then I was suddenly out, blinking in real light, warm as toast in my flimsy suit and boarding a truck. We went down out of the snowline and the shadows and into real heat and greenery. The mountains were almost blocked out by the buildings when we reached Bisho. The town hadn't changed much in nearly three years. The Head of Security Police looked much older though, and strangely unsure of himself. He looked away from my smile.

'Joseph,' he said. 'I have decided to take a big risk. You must understand that I am doing this without any authority from the Minister of the Interior. You are free to go.'

'OK,' I smiled.

'I want to warn you though.' The Head straightened his Sam Browne. 'There are still three counts of high treason against you. If you're ever caught committing an act of terrorism again that will be it. You will be executed. You will be hung. So go, and please don't ever let me see you again.'

'OK.' I think he saw every one of my teeth with the grin I gave. 'And thank you.'

I walked out of Bisho police headquarters free as a bird with a small sports bag holding my few possessions. Issued a travel warrant, I immediately caught the train to Transkei and Umtata station. From there I walked to my family home.

My two kids Sandile and Thandi seemed huge, different people. They were being looked after by my mother who appeared a lot older and sadder. She accompanied me to Angelinah's grave, then turned and stared.

'Zoleseli,' she said. 'I'm thankful you are out but please don't stay around here. Your aunts and I will take care of the children. I don't want any more trouble, you being arrested again like before.'

'Mama, that's all changed.' I smiled. But she was looking at the brown ground, not my face.

'You won't change, I know you. You break my heart. Leave us and go. Nobody wants you here.'

'Mama, look at me.' I tried, but it was no use. She would not meet my eyes.

'Transkei is at peace, no matter how hard we have it. You are a troublemaker. They all call you the Communist.'

'Mama,' I tried to take hold of her shoulders. 'That's all changed. I'm different. I'm back with God. I want to join a church.'

She shook free. 'Not you, Zoleseli. You're too clever, you're up to something again, we all know that. You want to join a church, do it away from here. Please.'

My smile slipped. Next day I left the Umtata area where I was so well known. I had decided my first priority was to find a church. But elsewhere in Transkei I found I was known. I would join a meeting but afterwards, enquiring about membership, I would notice looks given in the old tribal way. My reputation had preceded me. 'Not this one,' I saw a guy mouth at one church. I wandered round more churches in Transkei, which was after all my home. Again I got brick walls. Sometimes I got reasons. It would bring the Security Police around, having a convicted terrorist as a regular. They would harrass the rest of the congregation. Spies would be planted. Fear and suspicion would be sown. At the moment the churches were harmless to the regime. The Transkeian security police were different to the Ciskeian. Here, Kaiser Matanzima was still the Chief of the homeland and his police still had me targeted as a political animal, a leopard who could never really change his spots.

I absorbed some political knowledge after yet another rebuttal at another church. It was now 1983. Mandela was still alive and well and off Robben Island at last, but still a prisoner and moved to Pollesmoor further round the Cape. There had been a wave of ANC attacks on Boer cities outside the homelands. The war in Namibia was still raging with Angola invaded several more times. The South African military and the country itself was still headed by P. W. Botha.

In temporary accommodation, I decided to try and remove the cloud I was under. In formal terms befitting my university education, I wrote to government departments in Transkei and South Africa itself. I wrote to Kaiser Matanzima's office and that of the South African President. I wanted it put on record that Joseph Kobo was a changed man who only wanted a chance.

I remember as I posted a batch thinking, 'You wanted me, Lord, but who else does?'

I got no reply from the Transkeian authorities, but I got one from Pretoria. President P. W. Botha said yes, he would see me.

I went to Pretoria, the political capital of South Africa, by train. I had been granted a fifty-minute interview. I smiled. Botha was the former Minister of Defence in the seventies. He had been my direct opponent, I suppose, my arch enemy, head of the SADF and the organiser of the deployments in Namibia and Angola and the special forces' raids on the Frontline states, along with the border security I had so often infiltrated. He was actually known as 'The Crocodile' to the media. He would have all my files, of course, from 1963 to Kieskamahoek. I realised that I was involving the Ciskeian police chief on one hand, but on the other I was merely confirming the guy's judgement by my own action.

I arrived at the President's palatial office. The bodyguards must have shaken their heads as I appeared. They would have seen my file. Once I might have been ordered to infiltrate this very place with a view to assassination. Not now. I smiled when I was frisked. They would have found the old Joseph Kobo's Makarov in ten seconds flat. But I was unarmed. Escorted by Botha's private secretary, I was taken in to see the face I knew from a thousand photos and receive a far-from-icy handshake. The secretary whispered, 'Remember fifty minutes, Mister Kobo,' before retiring.

I was there in that room for two and a half hours.

P. W. Botha had read up on me all right. The man who was in charge of electrified border fences and atomic bombs made a few checks with my story and then surprised me.

Botha himself had once intended to be a church minister. He had been on the point of entering Bible college here in Pretoria when a by-election had suddenly occurred and he had been asked to stand as a National Party candidate. And then he had gone off down that track, ordering cross-border invasions to cut SWAPO supplies with me checkmating him in my own little way. Now both of us shared a pot of coffee and each learnt new things. Finally he pulled out a personal card.

'If what you say is true, Mr Kobo, and I believe it to be true, and you get into trouble with anyone, call me.'

The card had the phone number, private and official, of both him and his personal secretary. 'Any problems with anyone, plain policeman or general, give him my name. I'll back you. God has really touched you, Mr Kobo, hasn't He?'

I guess it is up to Mr Botha if he ever writes his memoirs to make a mention of that day, but I think he'll always remember it. I left with a big smile at the thought that I had the backing of the leader of white South Africa.

But now I realised it was essential to do something similar with the other camp. I had to explain myself to the ANC. I got in touch with old *Umkhonto* comrades and sure enough got summoned. And I got scared.

At least Botha had always been an enemy but I was going among friends and if it was realised that I was no longer with them I could be taken for a traitor and punished accordingly. I had God with me, but there was no way of proving that to a worldly political mind. I went to the *Umkhonto* base with far more trepidation than I had on the way to Pretoria.

The ANC had been fighting dirty wars and did not have unblemished hands. They had committed their excesses. They had executed their own. Like any military organisation the ANC had its brave soldiers and its downright psychopaths. It was geared up for wrongdoing in its ranks. The base I visited had its own detention barracks. Guards every bit as brutal as Boers frogmarched me before the base commander. I knew him well. I had last seen him at the Swaziland conference but he looked tired and even more angry. I'll call him Comrade 'A'. I smiled at him as he stood before an ANC flag and began:

'I'm very sorry, but you know my personal history. I was a minister of religion before 'sixty-three and God has called me back. I've got to obey Him.

214

I'm being quite open and honest. Nothing has
changed in my mind insofar as the political course
you guys are pursuing. I'm still one hundred per
cent with you in opposing oppression and
apartheid. It's worse than ever. Only God has
said I'm to work for Him only now. I can't work
for you any more, though you know all I've done
for you in the past.'

Comrade 'A' knew all right. He stared back
with his face a mask. I knew he had been Soviet-
trained like me. I ran through the night in
Kieskamahoek and then my return to Transkei and
my meeting with Botha. At that, the mask slipped
and the eyes widened. It occurred to me it might
have been unwise having visited the head of the
enemy before the ANC, but I could have cleverly
countered by saying that by doing in that way I
could have divulged no fresh information, had
they decided to arrest me and interrogate me about
the current leadership. I was after all three years
out of date now. Comrade 'A' did not make any
such challenge. He just stared. I could see things
in his eyes. Was I mad? Had that time in the
Drakensberg flipped me? Was I a security risk, or a
pathological liar, a double agent playing a very
clever game?

He took his time before answering. Even his
bodyguards started to fidget.

'All right,' he said. 'You wait. We'll check this
out, every last thing. Until then.' He nodded to

one of his men, a big Thembo-Xhosa with an ugly look.

I was taken to the base's detention barracks. It was not a pretty place. I heard beatings, screams, even shots. Disciplining was an ugly business. Informers, thieves, deserters, rapists, they were the same scum every army has had throughout history, no matter how good or bad its cause. I was at the moment scum too. I could see it. Word had quickly got around at the base and guys came for a look-see. I must gave been something of a legend but I could see grins or headshakes. This 'Comrade Miwe' who had done so much and had once been on the Executive wanted to throw it all away and serve the white guys' God.

Only I knew He wasn't the God of whites only.

I waited. The big Thembo guard was obviously an experienced enforcer. He stayed close to my cell. He wore a Makarov, just like the one I'd so often carried on missions. He would of course use his for the *coup de grâce* after the firing squad rifles. I waited in the cell, and of course prayed. I knew the ANC intelligence network was being utilised all across South Africa to get the truth, to detect the faintest whiff of a clever 'turning' operation by Security Branch. Even the Botha meeting would need to be confirmed. Two-and-a-half hours together sounded fishy, I knew. The Enforcer kept looking through my cell door with the Makarov under his arm.

One night I heard a man shriek nearby. He

was being tortured on suspicion of misusing funds.

His cell was empty when the Enforcer came for me and frogmarched me past.

Comrade 'A' was in his chair waiting, smoking a cigarette. He had received all the reports on my story, I knew. His eyes seemed clouded, as though allergic to his smoke. Then he blew out a perfect blue ring with his sigh. 'All right, Mr Kobo. All right. We in the ANC have nothing against anybody who wants to worship his God. The Movement advocates freedom of religion. If you have told us the truth then we have absolutely no right to keep you here. One thing, though. If we discover in due course that you were *not* telling the truth, then you know the consequences.' He nodded to his Enforcer. 'We'll come for you.'

The Enforcer was looking at him as though cheated. Comrade 'A' paused, then looked directly at me. 'Please . . . pray for *us*. Remember us who are still in our struggle, who haven't got our freedom, haven't found the sort of peace you appear to have. You remember us, Mister Kobo. Now go. Comrade-sergeant, escort him right out of base.'

The big Enforcer reluctantly did as he was told but stared hard after me. I hadn't been given any rank, nor had my codename been mentioned. I was no longer 'Comrade Miwe'.

I was free, but more the outcast than ever. I returned to the south, to Transkei, to try more churches and get more politely voiced reasons for being refused. But this time I had one friend. I

217

went to see a very old acquaintance, a long-retired black bishop, and explained the problem. He frowned. He had lost his clout but not his discernment.

'Well, why worry if churches won't accept you, Joseph? God has accepted you, forgiven you, restored you. All is well with you yourself, but if the church folk don't believe it, there is nothing you can do.' He saw my face fall but continued smiling. 'So the only thing you can do about it . . . is get out into the open. You don't need four walls and a roof. Just start work, Joseph. You know what to do, man. Preach. Find the toughest place to do it.'

The toughest place in the southeast was East London, especially its satellite township. It had always been a hard-boiled port of seamen and dockers. So I hit town, checked out the churches and offered help to local ministers. I hardly mentioned my name. I said nothing about my own pedigree—Bible college, university, ordained minister. I just helped. Politics flew in all directions but I ducked them easily.

I became more involved with the Independent black churches which had always been outsiders. Some were downright amateur, some dangerously so, confusing Christianity with the old ancestor-worship. Some places I visited were more like voodoo temples. Because of that I began to say and do things and forgot my caution. I corrected them, pointed out Scriptural accuracy. Guys did doubletakes at this nobody who knew something. Slowly, but surely I began to move up. I could talk to all sorts of people, from students to soldiers to hauliers to heavy drinkers; I had been all of these, of course. I was reordained. The rank of moderator was bestowed on me. I got used to the East London life, became a city slicker. And then I was leading young black pastors, helping train them, arranging for them to go to Bible college. I helped supply them. It was all slightly familiar. Then I was made a bishop. And then I got a call out of the blue.

I was wanted. A Mrs Sicwetch needed me. A Mrs who? The name was vaguely familiar. It was from way back in my past. It was going back around thirty years. Mrs Sicwetch was one of the mainsprings at that church in—where was it?— Lujizweni, where I had been probationary pastor. But that had been the fifties, and Mrs Sicwetch had been old then, born 1914 if I remembered right. And the place had been in the middle of nowhere, no water and no electricity, but I had been young and keen then. But this Mrs Sicwetch had not only remembered my name, she had never forgotten it. She had been praying for me all this time, since the early sixties when I had gone political. Now my name had loomed even larger, for I answered their need all of a sudden.

The Lujizweni church had themselves been branded outcasts. They had upset their hierarchy by becoming gripped by revival, praying and

219

fasting to incredible extremes. Praying for peaceful solutions to South Africa. Things that were weird in worldly eyes had happened as a result and in a very worldly way the Transkei Council of the Assembly of God had told the congregation to stop their hysteria. The Lujizweni congregation had been unable to obey and had gone on praying, holding services three times a day and fasting for weeks on end. The hierarchy had withdrawn their pastor, leaving the church leaderless. Mrs Sicwetch had prayed that bit harder and, without knowing anything about my guerrilla phase, had spoken my name.

A delegation from Transkei told me this, Mrs Sicwetch herself too old to travel far. I sat back in my comfy East London office and smiled, but shook my head. It couldn't be. It was nice to be remembered and to have featured in so many prayers, but I was a bustling-streets man now. I was sorry, but they had it wrong.

The very rustic delegation, some with blankets and sticks, returned home. Then they came back to say the same thing.

I was the one who had it wrong. They were sure. I was freshly amused and slightly irritated now. Look, I was doing fine here. My congregations were growing and there were sometimes visiting foreign seamen who added to the excitement. What did I want to go to the back of beyond for? Sorry, I said politely and watched them troop back to the train.

They came back a third time. Sorry, but it was me they wanted. Joseph Kobo was the guy and that was it. They'd keep coming unless . . . OK, I said. One visit. To see a few old faces.

We got onto the train. I doubled as the porter as I was the most able-bodied, carrying someone's stick for good measure. I thought maybe two days. A holiday, a break in the country. They had an evening service, as they had every evening. Having been thrown out of their old church building, they used someone's little hut. It was all very quaint and homely. And then the service began and they prayed and I listened to testimonies. I'd never seen such raw, wonderful faith. These folk were the poorest of the poor, scratching a living from the worst soil in South Africa, and the established church was treating them like actual dirt. Yet the things that were happening to these people, the clear-as-crystal miracles! People had been raised from the dead. Physical and emotional cripples had been healed. All this in the middle of nowhere. Someone should make it *somewhere*. Someone should definitely be guiding them, making sure they were rested and replenished in case they burnt themselves out, in short officering them. What kind of guy would do that?

'OK,' I said.

19

The Other Infiltrators

$\mathcal{N}$ot that I was the only South African who encountered things unexplained during the eighties.

One white guy was a second lieutenant—I'll call him 'B'—of the SADF. He had gained his commission as a conscript, such was his intelligence. He was university material, but he had done his duty. He and those closest to him were being threatened from the north by blacks. Not the blacks he had known, like his childhood nanny or the dustmen or the paperboys, but 'bad kaffirs'. He would rather have fought nobody and studied, but there was a need. If those insurgents got through, behind them would come Russians and Cubans eager to seize the Cape and cut the Western world in half.

The most dangerous border was South West Africa, or Namibia as outsiders called it. It was like the Israelis' Lebanon. The border had to be hermetically sealed and they had tried all through the seventies, but things had got worse by the time the second lieutenant had appeared. The old hands said it was like trying to stamp out bugs; more always came crawling out. With such comparisons, the war in South West Africa had got inevitably dirtier by the eighties. It had become a Vietnam. Despite a dozen more cross-border incursions like Cassinga, and dozens more clandestine supply-runs to SWAPO, there was a stalemate. Thousands had died but still SWAPO had its recruits, mainly from the Ovambo tribe.

Ovamboland was definite bandit country. Soldiers had got to hate the place, its heat and flatness with only palms to see. They had come to hate the people, seeing them as treacherous and two-faced, many of the smiling bowing daylight figures becoming attackers by night. And so My Lai-situations were inevitable. Ovambo villages known to be sympathetic to SWAPO were staked out, raided again and again and despite arrests, those same villagers would throw up new opponents.

Lieutenant 'B' was part of a swoop with Casspirs and Ratels on one such village. They were acting in fury. Some of their comrades had been caught in an ambush of the previous day, and it was known the culprits were local villagers. That sort of thing went through their mind. Soldiers in such conditions save all positive thoughts for one another. They get as close to fellow men as is healthily possible, almost love one another and would certainly lay down their lives.

224

It usually operates best at the smallest unit level, the ten-man squad or section.

Maybe some of Second Lieutenant 'B's comrades had been casualties in the nearby ambush. But he was angry and cold. His negative emotions were to the fore as he rode into their village. As a subaltern he had been responsible for a platoon, three-times-ten men. His idea of decency was for white soldiers and maybe some trusted blacks. But not the inhabitants of that village, men or women or even children. They were all the same. The women and children in his eyes were aiding the terrorists, hiding arms, transporting them, acting as scouts and spotters. His own CO was just as angry.

The village was to be razed. A collection of rondavels under the shade of trees, it was an easy target, although a careful approach was called for. Second Lieutenant 'B' spearheaded the attack, cutting his engine to coast in with total surprise. A few belts of tracer started the fires. Then belts of anti-personnel and grenades took over. Carriers raced in and smashed down huts. The gunners fired fast into the homes before anyone could appear, preferring not to view their victims directly. Soon the place was ablaze and all was quiet.

Not completely. Some soldiers pointed and an Ovambo child of two to three years appeared, wandering in a daze. His parents, or her parents, had been killed. The soldiers stared at their officer who shrugged.

Waiting in the Wing

'What do we do, sir? It's a flaming toddler.'

The subaltern looked around. The heat was unbearable. It was late, he wanted to have his men safely back in barracks. He stared around at the place. It was better to be thorough.

He gave an order, not looking at the tiny black figure.

'Sir?' a soldier asked.

The second lieutenant looked around. He could have leapt off his Casspir and been across to pick up the black child and have it safely in the cab, and maybe pass it on to trusted locals or an orphanage or hospital. But it was too much trouble. He was a soldier and his duty was to his men. He shrugged and nodded.

'Ja,' he said and dutifully picked up his command radio. The static hid the burst of gunfire and any sound of a cry.

The unit pulled back out of the village, having delivered the lesson to locals that it could be as ruthless as SWAPO. More patrols went on, including direct clashes with Cubans.

The nights in Namibia eventually became a memory to the second lieutenant.

He finished his term of conscription, returned to civilian life and a decent job, met a girl, married his sweetheart and, safe at last, settled down. Within the year the child was born, a healthy white baby. They had a joyful first birthday, and a second. But not a third. The toddler contracted a mysterious illness and within a few days died, just

226

short of his third birthday. The sobbing father remembered the Ovambo child whose execution he had allowed must have been almost exactly the same age. The veteran's wife said, 'Why? Why?'

The veteran did not answer.

The *Umkhonto* saboteur—who bore the same Christian name as me—did not answer for his atrocities. Joseph ran. When the bomb Joseph planted in a Port Elizabeth street went off and killed women and children, and a police crackdown quickly found his cell, he headed for a border. He drove his battered pickup across Cape Province and used the desert trick to enter Botswana, but he found a fullscale manhunt was on. The Boers knew who he was and where he might be headed and were closing off loopholes. Though they missed him at the border, they got one jump ahead by hitting ANC facilities inside Botswana and denying him sanctuary. The main Gaborone office was put out of action, as was another base at Francistown to the north. It was there that Joseph ditched the pickup and headed north on foot, hoping to hitch to the Zambian border. Botswanan police, with Boers at their shoulders, soon found the pickup and moved in pursuit. Realising roadblocks were ahead, Joseph turned off the main highway and entered the Chobe game reserve on foot. Avoiding wild animals and living off the land, he moved for a week and was within a day of Zambia when his luck changed.

A safari-party of South Africans were in the area and, skilled in hunting, they picked up traces of him. All the men in the party were army reservists and, hearing the radio alert, decided to have their own hunt. They went after Joseph's spoor as though tracking a wild animal. They caught him the same afternoon. The hunters called the police but not before they had posed proudly with their catch. In chains, Joseph was taken back to Francistown. His vehicle had been impounded but was needed back in South Africa for forensic evidence, for traces of bombmaking equipment and perhaps clues to other ANC. There was a problem. The vehicle was jury-rigged with its own starting motor and not even a police mechanic could start it. Joseph was pressed into driving his own vehicle back with, of course, a police escort.

A four-vehicle convoy moved south, with Botswanan and South African police. They were soon back on South African soil and headed for Pretoria, for judgement and probably a noose. But bad weather forced a detour through the Nelspruit region. Joseph found himself climbing a dizzy mountain pass, his armed guard at his elbow. It clicked he had a slim chance and little to lose. He raised his elbow, swung the wheel and took the pickup right off a hairpin bend and down a steep slope. It took a full minute to crash, by which time it had travelled two kilometres. The pickup was smashed to bits. The rest of the convoy, braking, scrambled down on foot. They found a dead policeman, but no Joseph.

He went on the run again for another Frontline state. Zimbabwe, as Rhodesia was now known, was too risky and the upper Limpopo too deep, so he headed due east for Mozambique. He got through, by infiltrating at the cutoff point of the live fence. He surrendered himself to Mozambican soldiers who took him to the ANC office in Maputo, the capital. Hearing his story, but unsure of the man himself, the local *Umkhonto* commander had Joseph put in detention barracks to check he was a genuine fugitive and not a Security Branch plant.

Days, weeks passed and still Joseph was an ANC prisoner. He decided to enlist powerful help. He was university educated and had a degree in English. He frenziedly wrote a letter in English to the wife of Nelson Mandela, still resident in Soweto at that time. He made a stupid mistake. Although the letter was a simple plea for her intervention in his case, he addressed it in the name of Mandelson, the English version of Mandela. It was a harmless mistake but again at that time the ANC bases in Mozambique were being infiltrated by RENAMO as well as Boer forces. The local commissar assumed Joseph had sent out a secret code to a white contact. He was given a summary court martial and sentenced to be executed in a nearby clearing.

Two enforcers marched him out at gunpoint

where he was forced to dig his grave, still protesting total innocence. A third enforcer appeared to perform the execution with an RPD machine gun while one of the others effected the *coup de grâce*. By now Joseph was in a state of hysteria, the victim of closed minds and paranoia. He started to cry for help, and then the newly arrived executioner took a close look at him. He recognised him. They were from the same kraal and the same clan in the Transkei, though they had joined the ANC at different times. The executioner came to a swift decision and decided blood was paramount. He whispered a plan to Joseph. They went through the moves of the execution until the very last second when the RPD swung onto the two other enforcers. The second man survived, but Joseph closed and turned the man's own pistol on him.

The two kinsmen realised they were marked men. They bolted for it, heading for nearby Malawi which, though a black state, was rigidly anti-Frontline. From there, skirting Zambia which they knew would have enforcement teams on the lookout, they slipped into Zaire, another non-Frontline state. In the capital Kinshasa they walked into a Scandinavian embassy and told their story. They were granted asylum and flown out on a UN passport to Sweden, where they were accorded the status of political exiles. Joseph and his kinsman found themselves standing alongside other South Africans of Boer origin, young men who had fled to avoid service in the SADF and who also sought a new life.

One of the most closely guarded lives in South Africa was that of Chief Kaiser Matanzima, ruler of the Transkei and a person evoking comparisons with Pétain and Vikun Quisling. He had a large group of bodyguards around him at all times. All were black but had received training in South Africa and were topnotch protectors. Both Matanzima's official residence and his vast private farm were garrisoned round the clock for fear of attack by ANC guerrillas. The bodyguards were equipped with the best equipment, courtesy of Pretoria, such as R4 rifles and M79 launchers. They also had a unit of South African special forces on standby should there be a major attack on the Chief. Only verbal attacks had occurred through the sixties and seventies, and still Matanzima was in total power, though the bodyguards maintained their vigil.

One afternoon a local bus drew up outside the Matanzima farm and two passengers got out. The guards identified the first as one of Matanzima's wives, not accorded the privilege of a car and returned from a brief holiday. There was another woman also of the black race right behind her. She looked hesitant and humble and the bodyguards assumed it was the wife's maid. It was a hot afternoon and they were watching for more sinister signs, the glint of metal on a ridge or the flash of telescopic glass. The wife with the second woman following was allowed inside and both in their sedate African way walked up the long drive to the house, past more bodyguards.

Inside, Chief Matanzima and one of his family, his brother in point of fact, were relaxing in no little luxury. With the wife's arrival they both got up and then all three turned to look at the new woman who came in her wake. The stranger still looked humble but she was carrying something. It was not a hand-grenade or a snub-nosed gun. It was a message. She was not an ANC or PAC agent carrying out ruthless orders. She was a member of the tiny Lujizweni church and had been chosen to tell Chief Matanzima, mightiest man in the homelands, that God would *depose* him unless he repented of all the sins he had carried out against his fellow blacks. Moreover, the best bodyguards in the country, who would have opened fire on even a woman had they realised she was an infiltrator, had opened all the doors for her to do it.

Her name was Margaret Nvqancashe and she had been told what to do in a vision, although her invasion of the guarded farm had been done in total innocence. 'Mama Margaret' as the fellow-members of her congregation knew her, had never harmed a soul in her life and, with a completely clear conscience and doing God's bidding, had been allowed a completely clear run. This incident had been at the very start of the eighties. Even before I appeared, the name of tiny Lujizweni church had been on the lips of my oldest opponent.

20

Soldiers of the King

So I went on into the nineties with just the one
base, after the dozens of hides I had known.
Lujizweni was a kraal so small it never appeared
even on the largest-scale maps. Nothing of importance had happened there, except for the killing of
a white missionary in the 1830s. He had apparently been a German, landed with the British, the
third wave of whites. The savagery of the incident
is at odds with the scenery. The Lujizweni area is a
calm place with which Western visitors easily identify; for an Englishman it resembles the Cotswolds,
for an Irishman County Down and for an
American New England, though with something of
an Oklahoman Indian reservation. There had been
a curious historical footnote to that missionary's
murder in that the local sub-tribe, the Pondos, had
been the only one in South Africa that hadn't
waited to be re-missionaried. They had actually
gone out and bought a Bible, one of the very few
English-language Bibles in the country in the early
nineteenth century. To purchase this Bible they

had given an elephant's tusk, an extremely prized commodity. So it was as though the people of the area had gone out and got the Good News all by themselves.

People like Mama Margaret and Mrs Sicwetch were among the torchbearers of that purchase. They had never forgotten the Bible, never stopped believing, before and after my fifties pastorship. They had never doubted God was the answer to every single problem, all through the township crises and the ANC bombings. They had prayed for healing in things big and small, for people they knew and total strangers. And afflicted locals had been healed and the black-versus-white bloodbath in South Africa had not occurred, despite the hangings on one side and the 'necklacings' on the other and the domino-falls of Angola, Mozambique and Zimbabwe.

When I first joined in the prayers at the little church I was still worldly enough to believe I had more knowledge than my congregation. I knew that in an all-out conflict the Boers would still make mincemeat of blacks, but after my meeting with P. W. Botha I could understand why they might do it. They had every reason to feel a terror at being swamped, overrun if they allowed freedom to all South Africans. They had behaved badly but so had all the other white rulers around them, except when colonialism collapsed and they were the ones left out on a limb holding on tight and occasionally having to climb down to perform surgery to keep the tree intact. I understood that. I understood why even a liberally-minded white guy would stiffen when he heard these 'Kill-the-Boer' chants and why he would keep his gun handy. I realised he had had good reason to suspect the Sino-Cuban-Soviet presence in all the Frontline states.

It was at the very end of the decade that my mind stopped working cleverly and I looked in renewed astonishment at those praying around me. Mrs Sicwetch ignored my gaping jaw and just went on smiling, crying, fasting and praying. That was the time when, just when it seemed the South African domino was about to be played, all the players' hands were *held*. Russia's own set of dominoes began to fall in Afghanistan, breaking up all the way back to the Berlin Wall and Cuba. China, too, had sudden dissident problems. It very quickly came about that these countries could no longer afford the luxury of abundantly supplying people like the ANC, who now found themselves on a limb of sorts.

For the more rabid insurgents it meant that their dream of leading a southward invasion complete with T54s and Migs would never be realised. On the other side of the coin, the collapse of the Communist threat meant the SADF could no longer really proclaim themselves as southern defenders of the Free World. It also meant that the majority of apolitical South Africans would be less pressured, that Mandela and the ANC were not necessarily bogeymen or updated Mau-Mau or anti-Christs. The more sinister elements with the ANC were actually *less* sinister now. The waters seemed less muddied.

At that time in 1990 plenty of military strategists must have been blinking and rethinking. Mrs Sicwetch and her congregation just smiled and prayed. Very soon after had come Namibia, Namibia electing a SWAPO government which was making peace with the local whites. It was emulating Zimbabwe, which had had ten years of such co-operation. One can wonder whether ZANLA and SWAPO, forced once to operate from Mozambique and Angola, had also been forced to witness the real results of a white exodus and understand compromise. Which would be a matter for Robert Mugabe and Sam Nujoma to state and not Joseph Kobo.

What I will state is that passage from the Bible, 1 Corinthians 2:6–7:

> We do, however, speak of a message of wisdom among the mature, but not the wisdom of . . . the rulers of this age, who are coming to nothing. No, we speak of God's secret wisdom, a wisdom that has been hidden and that God destined for our glory before time began.

The rulers at the time that was written, the rulers of Corinth and the known world, were

Romans and they fell completely and irredeemably; I should know with my birth in the year a modern Caesar tried to revive that Empire, remember. The Bible still has everything you need to know and the nineties simply reiterate it. All the 'isms' have proved flawed, from Marxism to racism to separatism. Oh, the Bible has been misused and twisted, sure, but men have done that. It's as strong as it was right back in Roman times when the only known crocodiles swam in the Nile. And at a time when the Jews were calling for a military solution to Roman rule. When Jesus came among them He refused that solution, to their outrage. His disciples were not a military wing. The ones who did take up armed struggle, the Zealots, were quickly surrounded and slowly crushed at Masada. And a later Masada was of course Rome itself.

There is a moment in Prokofiev's 'Dance of the Knights' from the *Romeo and Juliet Suite*—I got to like Russian composers after Moscow and Odessa—where the stirring martial theme slows and the whole tune becomes faintly ridiculous, the duellists turn elephantine. So it should be. For all my military training, gun-stripping to minelaying, I know military glory must not be kept gleaming. There can be a time for it. I had nearly four years in all-out guerrilla warfare—which is the usual span of all-out effort. The real fighting in both world wars was around four years. More, and things crumble. It took around four years for both the Russians and Americans to realise they were not going to win their Asian conflicts. Well, '76 to '80 is how long I lasted. I was saved in two ways. I rediscovered the Lord's presence and I was spared from being killed.

In all probability had I returned to terrorism in the eighties and been rearrested, I would, after that police chief's warning, have been finished off. Or been forced into a shootout. But I at last listened to the Lord. And when I reread the Bible I of course found so much in the Joseph of Genesis, his imprisonment, his coat of many colours like my camouflage suit, his making things right with his brothers and discarding grudges, maybe even his living to a hundred and ten—we'll see. I also found a lot in the Book of Jonah, running from God's will, going overseas and encountering close shave after shave and finally being spat out of imprisonment. Most of all, though, the Lord's question to him: 'Have you any right to be angry?'

At the time I had the right, I thought. But I was spared having to shoot in anger, or even in cold blood.

I got out of that. And got love out of it. I learnt, after all my hand-to-hand combat training, that the ultimate way to disarm a man is to love him. Love has the greatest weaponry. You love a man to death. The lowminded black guy chanting 'We'll be the bosses now' and the hardskinned Boer stormtrooper explosively facing him—they might both say 'stupid woman' and shoot at you, but

238

neither will feel a hundred per cent hate, not if they're real men.

And women. I remember once comparing womanliness with a policeman's punches—I love women more than ever. Which brings me to another thing I got out of love. The romantic version. I got me a wife again. Mabel, her name is, and she is the daughter of none other than Mrs Sicwetch. So that grand old lady, born 1914, not only got herself a pastor but a son. My love for Mandela had also grown and when he was finally released in February 1990 and he smiled at the world, you could see the love in him. All the time he was being held, South African history was being held with him. While the rest of the world had changed, men had too. The leaders of all the Frontline states had changed during the eighties— Khama in Botswana, Numeiri in the Sudan, Nyerere in Tanzania, Kaunda in Zambia, Neto in Angola, Machel in Mozambique, Smith's successor Muzorewa in Rhodesia-Zimbabwe, Jonathan in Lesotho, Dlamini in Swaziland and of course Botha here in South Africa.

And all that time Mandela was made to wait. A man who in 1963 was forty-six, the same age as the legendary JFK, my other idol. And yet had John Kennedy escaped assassination he would only have been eligible for one more term of office and would not have made the eighties, far less the nineties. Whether his surviving would have prevented Vietnam or his family would have retained

dynastic control of America until the present day is
mere speculation, but the fact is that Kennedy himself would have been past history.

The focus of history has now come back to
Mandela. And see how much was burnt off him in
the meantime. Just like it was burnt off me. In a
cell your rage can't get through the door so it
bounces back at you until you get new angles.
Maybe you even understand how the guy on the
other side of the door is feeling. The same man,
when you are released, will open the door that bit
more readily if he feels the guilty one.

That guy Dumas—whom I always liked,
besides the factor of his having a black grand-
mother—had his Count of Monte Cristo going
ahead and settling scores with those who had
without doubt wronged him. But in destroying
them he destroyed himself. All his learning and
planning and waiting and he blew it. He lost. All
he did was put on his enemies' clothes and become
like them. He thought he had earned the right to
revenge when in fact he had won his education, his
means of escape and his treasures from his
cellmate, who was a man of God. The avenger had
thus been given a chance to know God's way and
refused it.

It is a fact that almost every player in the sub-
Saharan conflict knew God from the start. The
Frontline state leaders aided each other not so
much because of a diabolical conspiracy, but
because they had been students together. They

had nearly all studied in South Africa. The universities there, even with apartheid, were the best in the whole continent and everyone knew it. So Mandela, Mugabe, Kaunda, Nyerere—even Portuguese subjects from Angola and Mozambique—were personal acquaintances from further education. Furthermore, each had received his primary education from Christian missionaries, so all of them when kids had known about Christ. It's true. The old theory of the British Empire's demise goes that for all its military bearing, it also sowed the seeds of self-destruction by promoting Christianity, for it was those values that eventually worked their way to the surface to cause guilt and shame. Such seeds should blossom. Those African leaders, whether they became socialist or fascist or Marxist, had the seeds in them. They knew something, even if they did nothing about it. Jonah, even when still imprisoned, said, 'Those who cling to worthless idols forfeit the grace that could be theirs.'

Mandela was brought up a Methodist, but any more about the seed in him is his story. It is not for his kinsman Joseph Kobo to put words into his mouth or take words out. More than ever I would give my life for him and Mandela is my hero, my tribal prince uncle, but he is still only a man. I know who my King is and He lives for ever. I *did* take from Mandela, though. Using Lujizweni church as our jumpoff, we planted a mass of sister churches, just like in his 'M' plan with street cells.

We planted over a hundred new churches and covered hundreds of miles as the calendar moved towards the nineties. The 'M' plan was always a good plan. It worked well. We soon had with each church a congregation numbering anything from fifty to three thousand people, a membership of close on half a million. The churches though were and are mainly tents. But those same churches have gone on multiplying and leaping right across Transkei and over its borders, to Lesotho and East London and Natal, and further.

One of the farthest-flung new churches is in Namibia. In Ovamboland, the old battleground between the SADF and SWAPO for over two decades, a certain pastor is well loved by the local tribes. The pastor is a white South African who before being ordained was a military man and was very familiar with the region. He was Second Lieutenant 'B'.

Mama Margaret Nvqancashe who penetrated the heavily guarded home of Chief Kaiser Matanzima, Premier of Transkei, to implore him to change his ways before God, is still in my church. She was allowed to leave the Matanzima farm unharmed that time in 1980, though her advice was not heeded. In 1990, ten years later, Matanzima *was* deposed after he and his family were found guilty of massive corruption.

It would be tempting to think that another church has been planted right out of Africa and as far north as you can get. In Scandinavia, my namesake Joseph, the guy who shot his way out of an ANC base in Mozambique with a kinsman, now has a high-flying job. He holds an executive position in the steel industry. He owes that position to a good education which he in turn owes to a missionary education, though whether he thanked the Lord for all his miraculous escapes across half a dozen countries is for him to announce. Maybe he remembers the biblical Joseph's story, raised to exalted rank in an alien country before making his peace. Steel is a good line to be in, especially if it's weathered the recession, though I know more about irony.

One example is the South African army having very much copied the tactics of the Israeli Defence Force, especially in the all-points-of-the-compass incursions, and yet the father of the IDF having been the military wing of the Jewish underground of the forties, a wing Mandela freely admitted was his model for *Umkhonto*. Another irony—in Transkei a homeland special forces unit is raised for security reasons, an all-black unit. Their chief instructor is a man of proven experience, a white Zimbabwean who in the seventies had commanded our most formidable enemies, the Selous Scouts. It's true—smile. I did.

There is too much common ground, and there is too much ground anyway in South Africa. A big country should be for a similarly-sized people. When guys yell about killing the Boers or play off tribes against each other in the old imperial way or, most ironic of all, demand their own homelands, they are doing the place down. To scrap the old Bantustan system and have Transkei and all the others back in the Republic, as is promised, will be wonderful, one of the best first moves. I wouldn't want the white guys to be making their own moves out, no matter what wild minds might want. As a trained economist I know that a white exodus would be terrible. Economics, in the form of the international banks, played a key role in forcing Pretoria to go the right way.

Should white people then go on living in their sumptuous houses with their adjacent pools? Why not? But surely only if they pay their workers and servants properly so they too might move upward. If that proves financially wrong, it shows how impossible it was in the first place. You simply have to cut your cloth. Better cutting cloth than throats. Better counting out pennies than rounds of ammunition. Better, as that walking political contradiction Churchill said, to jaw than war.

So what about this guy Kobo . . . now a harmless ex-warhorse out to pasture? Everything clean and easy now? No, I get even more frightened now and I get literal blood on my hands.

I got frightened that time in my church when I touched the woman who had died from a massive haemorrhage hours before, after folk pleaded with me to try and revive her. She was clinically dead. She had bled to death. I had turned my head away as I touched her and prayed. Then I looked up to find everyone staring, not at me but past me. She was up, back to life. Healed. And still alive today. And the group of boys in shorts and bare feet who came in with their friend in a wheelchair. It was no joke—he was a lifelong cripple. I prayed and touched him and out he got, shakily at first. He needed to be half-carried out but soon his legs were getting stronger and he was out on the veldt within a short while, playing stick-fencing and football. And seeing the people strolling out when they had been brought in as lunatics, leashed or roped. And meeting the bunch of black builders who appeared out of the blue to construct a real church for nothing, a building we now use and which I intend as the blueprint for turning our hundred sister churches from tents into bricks-and-mortar. We also intend to put up a monument of some kind at the scene of that first missionary's murder all those years ago.

Maybe you think I've been brainwashed, like before. You bet I am, *now*. But I was never previously indoctrinated, in a Frontline state or on the Black Sea. We weren't stupid. We knew the Soviets wanted to seal a devil's bargain and it suited us to play along, a means to an end only. But there was no bargaining necessary with God, despite His wait. Believe me, this is a tough guy talking. I've not got weak like those warders I used to taunt. It's got much tougher. Running services every day, running people around, housing them, keeping up links here and overseas . . . it's like logistics with a capital 'L'.

It has always taken tough guys to live in South Africa, tough as the Boers when they formed their laager against overwhelming odds, tough as guys marooned for thirty years and still smiling. South Africa has enough wild animals; men should be different. They shouldn't be in packs or prides.

For me it's been irony and adversity. They say nothing succeeds like success, but only for so long. Unchecked success gives rise to arrogance and a belief in one's own destiny. In military terms, you tell soldiers they are special, they are the elite and they'll believe it and do superhuman things for a while. It's good to aim for high standards and get so trained, but when such a unit starts being superior to everyone else around, it gets dangerously Nazi. The SADF are a superb army but it took that repulse at Cuito Cuanavale in Angola in 1988 to show them solutions by military means aren't plain sailing. Some would say needing adversity is a stumbling-block to people who are going places. I'd say there are only two places you can go in the long run. Heaven or Hell. I well remember mentioning them in the middle of a furious moment torn between staying a docile churchman or joining the armed struggle. To someone trying to reason with me, I rounded with the words, 'I'd rather be free in Hell than a slave in Heaven.'

I got it wrong. Take it from an African, there are no slaves in Heaven. At the time I was ready to sell my soul if it meant freedom for my people, like a lot of black guys were. But to me, God said, 'No need.' There was and is no need for anyone to die like that for this country, whether they themselves kill for some cause, whether they assassinate Communist leaders or yes, even murder in a church.

South Africa, the world in one country, has a lot more world to let in. I've maybe got a start on that for I keep going abroad and back. I travel more and more. I've seen much more of England and the United States, leaving and returning to Lujizweni, preaching and sometimes telling snippets of my story. No need to slip across borders now; I have a valid South African passport, but no more VIP lounges although my message is the most important of all. In Britain my main base is in Essex. All my forestry knowledge—hardwood, softwood—but I'd never heard of Brentwood until then. And I've preached in nearly every church that side of the British capital. I sometimes get confused about which East London I'm in. Having been to the west coast of America, including Disneyland, I've a great idea for a theme park in South Africa. There's a place you could rename as 'Treasure Island' after the Disney adaptation of the Stevenson story. You could easily get families out on the short trip from the mainland. Otherwise, Robben is going to stand unused and unwanted.

On the mainland, I still drive as much as I can, and I know drivers more than most folk get antagonistic because they're in entrenched positions that don't allow proper communication, so you misread intentions and think the worst of one another. The trick is to stop and talk before any crash.

At the Rustenberg Conference of 1990 the South African Churches all got together, properly at last, and three bishops of the Dutch High Reformed church stood up and said something that wasn't scriptural, but almost as wonderful. They said, 'Sorry.' I was there to see it.

I wasn't there on 16 December 1993 when Mandela, wearing a camouflage suit, went to a stadium and formally stood the *Umkhonto we Sizwe* down, recognising the part it had played in South African history. There should be no need for a re-mobilisation with a genuine SADF in the making. A lot of the *Umkhonto* guys who were there will be SADF officers. Some are already away being trained in England, at Sandhurst. They'll learn to be gentlemen, professionals imbued with chivalry, and yet the elite of even the British army are their special forces, who ironically train like guerrillas. They asked me to come to the stand-down that day. They said I deserved some rank or recognition despite my change of spots. I told them I've got all the rank I want.

Despite my bishop's status I still come under attacks. I found myself being charged by a white in Pretoria, just after I had finished preaching at a Dutch High Reformed church. It was like a rhino coming in, animal *or* armoured car.

'Kobo. You, Joseph Kobo!' I heard the

challenge and turned slowly from the service sheet.
I could hear the running feet. 'I heard all you said,
telling me about your past, and you know what
you are?'

A Boer lady of about seventy in the standard
uniform of wide sunhat, floral dress, handbag and
high-heeled shoes seemed about to spear me with
a parasol. I tried to smile but her eyes were red.

'You know! All your talk! If there's one man I
could never ever stand it was that Nelson
Mandelson!' She used the Anglicised name. 'All
those years, thirty years I couldn't. And now you
say I've got to pray for him, that he makes the right
moves, picks the right people, does the right thing?
You know what you are, Joseph Kobo?' I saw she
was red with tears rather than rage. 'You are *right*.
To think my family's here three hundred and fifty
years and I've got to pray for a black man.
Goodbye, Bishop!'

Then she was away, clickclacking back up the
aisle before I could say a single word. I noticed
that her eyes had really been of the softest blue,
like sky over mountains or ocean. The hush that
had fallen around me was still there, so I could
hear the rumble of a heavy vehicle outside, a
Casspir by its engine-tone, which meant troops
heading east back to barracks, maybe the airforce
barracks on Church Street which had been car-
bombed in 1983. I heard the Casspir driver gently
drop a gear. Maybe he was slowing to allow the
lady across the road. I guess she now knew that

this building she had probably always worshipped in was more important than any barracks. I heard the brakes and then an impatient rev as the Casspir reluctantly stopped. It revved again, with the old lady obviously tired after her charge at me and taking her time. I should have gone out and told that army driver it was well worth the wait.

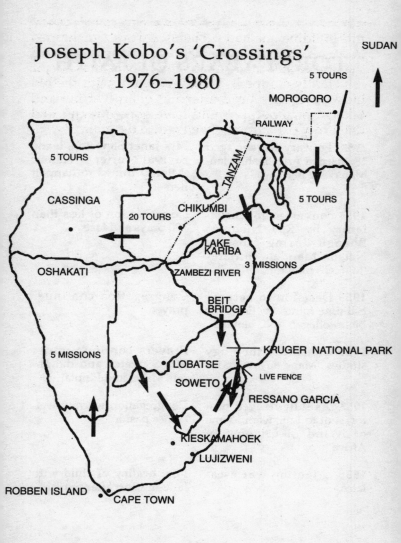

Joseph Kobo's 'Crossings'
1976–1980

SUDAN

5 TOURS

MOROGORO

RAILWAY

5 TOURS

TANZAM

CASSINGA

CHIKUMBI

20 TOURS

LAKE KARIBA

3 MISSIONS

OSHAKATI

ZAMBEZI RIVER

BEIT BRIDGE

KRUGER NATIONAL PARK

5 MISSIONS

LOBATSE

SOWETO

LIVE FENCE

RESSANO GARCIA

KIESKAMAHOEK

LUJIZWENI

ROBBEN ISLAND

CAPE TOWN

FORTY YEARS OF FAITH

JOSEPH KOBO

1953 Forestry worker aged 18, married Angelinah. Mau-Mau rising in Kenya.

1954 converted to Christianity by Rev Nicholas Bhengu during crusade. Nelson Mandela initiates 'M' (cell) plan for ANC.

1955 Decision to become full-time minister. Enrols at Bible college. ANC banned.

1956 Continues theology studies. Mandela arrested.

1957 As fully-fledged pastor, sent to Lujizweni. Time of 'Wind of Change' in Africa.

1958 Algerian war escalates.

LUJIZWENI

Mrs Janet Sicwetch, leads revival after vision. 'Mighty things to happen here'.

Congregation of less than 100 prays and fasts.

Congregation continues prayer.

Prayers continue under Mrs Sicwetch and daughters Mabel and Pumla.

Congregation warmly welcomes pastor.

First healing of child with hole-in-heart after prayer.

1959 Urban terrorist tactics in Algeria.

Second healing. Girl with internal damage successfully prayed for.

1960 Sharpeville massacre. 69 blacks shot dead.

Prayers and fasting for peace and reconciliation.

1961 Transferred to pastor in towns. ANC forms military wing, *Umkhonto we Sizwe*.

Farewells.

1962 Pastors in cities. Mandela and first *Umkhonto* cadres undergo guerrilla training abroad.

Congregation includes Joseph Kobo in prayers.

1963 Mandela rearrested on sabotage charges. Transkei among so-called 'homelands'. JFK assassinated.
  Breaks with church, renounces Christianity.

"

1964 Full-time political activist in Transkei. Mandela on Robben Island. War breaks out in Portuguese Africa.

"

1965 Becomes secretary to UDF (umbrella organisation for ANC-affiliated movements). Rhodesia declared UDI.

"

1966 Verwoerd assassinated. Given 90-day detention including torture.

Congregation includes Joseph Kobo in its prayers.

1967 Leaves SA to study at LSE, England. Chief Luthuli, head of ANC, mysteriously killed.

"

1968 Continues study in London. Americans stall in Vietnam.

"

1969 Returns to SA. Arrested and shipped to Robben Island.

"

1970 Robben Island.

"

1971 Released. Amin in power in Uganda.

"

1972 Rearrested.

"

1973 Joins ANC delegation to UN in New York. Promoted in political wing.

"

1974 Rearrested. Collapse of Portuguese Africa.

"

1975 Continues activism. Neto and Machel, leaders in Angola and Mozambique, offer haven to ANC.

"

1976   Soweto killings. Hundreds of school children die.   Decides to take up armed struggle, joins ANC military wing. Exfiltrates SA.

Congregation includes Joseph Kobo in its prayers.

1977   Commissioned, trained in Frontline states and Soviet Union. Begins 'crossings'.

"

1978 Sees action in Angola, Rhodesia. More 'crossings'.

"

1979   More 'crossings'. Promotion within *Umkhonto*.

"

1980   Imprisoned in Drakensberg mountains. Rhodesia   becomes Zimbabwe. Neto of Angola dies. Amin toppled.

Member of congregation Margaret Nvqancashe visits Transkei Premier after vision.

1981 Remains imprisoned. ANC begin urban attacks within SA.

Congregation includes Joseph Kobo in its prayers.

1982 Remains imprisoned. SA special forces make incursions into Frontline states.

Prayers   and   fasting increase. Disapproval from church hierarchy.

1983   Informed wife Angelinah   has   died. Undergoes dramatic return to Christianity,   renounces armed struggle. Meets Botha. Numeiri deposed in Sudan.

Hierarchy warns congregation to 'desist' in revival.

1984 Returns to Transkei but seen as dangerous terrorist. Made an outcast.

Congregation deprived of ministers, then church building. Continues prayers. Made outcasts. Uses ordinary house.

1985 Contacted by Lujizweni. Agrees to return as pastor. Russia stalls in Afghanistan.

Warmest of welcomes. Marries Mabel.

1986 Machel of Mozambique killed.

Initiates plan for sowing sister churches across SA, not unlike 'M' plan.

1987 Leads prayers. Healings increase. Increasing unrest in SA, especially Natal.

Twenty new sister churches in Transkei. Contacts UK churches.

1988 Stalemate in Angola after Cuito Cuanavale. Mass unrest across SA.

New church built. More sister churches. Contacts US churches.

1989 Berlin Wall falls.

More sister churches, beyond Transkei.

1990 Mandela released. Free elections in Namibia. SWAPO wins.

Healings multiply. Transkei premier deposed.

1991 More churches reaped.

Seventy sister churches.

1992 More churches reaped.

Multiple healings. Eighty sister churches.

1993 *Umkhonto we Sizwe* decommissioned. *Waiting in the Wing* written.

One hundred sister churches and still counting. Prayers with a capital 'P' for everyone in South Africa.